HOW TO RESTORE
Suspension and Steering

OSPREY
RESTORATION
GUIDE 12

HOW TO RESTORE

Suspension and Steering

Roy Berry

Published in 1987 by Osprey Publishing Limited
27A Floral Street, London WC2E 9DP
Member company of the George Philip Group

Sole distributors for the USA

Osceola, Wisconsin 54020, USA

British Library Cataloguing in Publication Data

Berry, Roy
  How to restore suspension and steering.
  —(Osprey restoration guide; 12)
  1. Automobiles—Maintenance and repair
  I. Title
  629.28'722   TL152
ISBN 0-85045-715-7

Editor Tony Thacker

Filmset by Tameside Filmsetting Limited,
Ashton-under-Lyne, Lancashire
Printed by BAS Printers Limited,
Over Wallop, Hampshire, Great Britain

CONTENTS

Introduction

People embark on the restoration of a car for several reasons. The professional restorer does it to make money, either as a speculative 'earner' or as paid work for someone else. It is much more difficult to discover why an amateur takes on a restoration. It may be nostalgia for a particular vehicle—the possibility of owning and running the once coveted and unattainable. It may be for the pleasure in the craft of restoration or in anticipation of the satisfaction of using the finished car. In most cases it's probably a little of all these reasons. As an amateur, you may not be as concerned financially as the professional, but if you are astute in the choice of car, the price you pay for it and the management of the restoration, you can be sure that you will be on the 'right side' in the end.

How does the restoration of steering or suspension fit into all of this? When I was a mechanic in a garage, I generally did not like this sort of work. Most of it was done under the vehicle, and tight king pins in a beam axle or shackle pins on a leaf spring could entail a lot of slogging with a big hammer and often blooded knuckles. Seldom was there time to clean things enough to make subsequent work enjoyable. What is different about a restoration? Well, it depends how you do it. You will see in chapter 8 that some suspension units can be removed quite easily (there are, for example, six attachment bolts on some Jaguars). If your car comes into this category and you are restoring rather than making running repairs, then this is the way to do it. Working on a bench is *much* nicer than under the car, and is also much safer. When the suspension is off, you can dismantle it in comfort and clean, paint and rebuild it thoroughly. The E type rear suspension on our cover, with new bushes, pins, bearings, springs, nuts and bolts, gives an idea of what can be achieved.

Where the finished car is concerned, I have often quoted a friend, Lionel Burrell of *Classic Cars* magazine, who says that what the enthusiast is interested in for his restored car is 'what it looks like, what it feels like and what it goes like'. One of the most disappointing aspects of driving or riding in restored cars is that they often do not feel as good as they did when new. In some cases the reason might be nothing more than an unwise choice of tyres—modern ones do not suit old suspensions—but, sadly, it is sometimes deeper-rooted. The car may drift or pull to one side, pitch on a bumpy road, or wallow on a bend. From a performance point of view, the ability to put down the power, keep the car on line through a bend and brake it sensitively or quickly depends on keeping the tyres in contact with the road—the province of the suspension. In terms of on-the-road satisfaction, precise steering in response to sensible effort at the wheel, enabling you to judge the road surface and feel in contact, is very reassuring.

From the economic point of view, doing the steering and suspension yourself will obviously save money, and if the finished car really does handle and ride as it should, this will be a big point in its favour when you come to sell it.

I have included a simple introduction to the technology and theory of steering and suspension in chapter 2. Knowing something about why your car behaves in a certain way will be useful in diagnosing faults and, if you feel so inclined, experimenting with steering and suspension angles. With one or two exceptions, though, there is little to be gained and probably more to be lost in the latter course of action, which might also prove dangerous.

Work carefully when you are under the car, supporting it on stands or that old-fashioned but excellent alternative of good square blocks of wood (*not* masonry or bricks). When jacking and supporting the car remember that it too can be harmed, in fact seriously damaged, by careless jacking. The Jaguar E type and the Aston Martin DB 2/4, for example, have lightweight tubular chassis at the front which are strong as structures but are easily damaged by the sort of point-load imposed by a jack or an axle stand.

Use a piece of wood on the jack, or a substantial piece of timber spanning two axle stands, to spread the load.

When you have completed the work, take the car to a competent garage to have its front-end geometry checked. Too many people take a chance on this. The satisfaction you get from an old car which steers and rides as it ought will repay the work you put into it.

In writing this book I have called on the help of a number of people. For this I would like especially to thank Guy Scott, Howard Payne, Ian Berry, Robert Tappin, Roger Cadnam, Amanda Wright, Alastair Thomas, Paul Gough, Peter Green, and June Whitaker, who did the typing; the following companies who have kindly given me permission to reproduce diagrams from their manuals: British Leyland, Jaguar Cars and Aston Martin Lagonda Ltd. Special thanks, too, to *Classic Cars* magazine, where some of the photographs used here were previously published, and to Vic Hillier who has allowed me to use, in chapter 2, some illustrations from his book *Fundamentals of Motor Vehicle Technology*. Lastly, I have to thank my wife, Penny, for her steadfast support and for the production of the photographs and many of the diagrams.

Roy Berry
January 1987

Chapter 1 | Some essential preliminaries

As an enthusiast contemplating the restoration of your car's suspension and steering, you are likely to have some previous experience of car repairs, already own a basic tool kit and have somewhere in which to work. With this in mind, I will concentrate here on the necessary extras for the task.

A prime consideration is personal safety. Obviously if a car weighing between one and two tonnes falls on you, it will do a lot of harm! A firm, level floor is essential, as is a set of robust axle stands which will give you a reasonable space in which to work. I prefer the three-legged variety as those with four legs need to be used on a really flat floor to be stable. The serious restorer will make life easier by buying a good trolley jack with a substantial lifting height and plenty of lifting capacity. I use one which will lift two tonnes to a height of some 50 cm, giving me a margin of safety and space.

When you are working on the suspension and steering you will spend a lot of time lying underneath the car, so it is a good idea to make yourself comfortable. Creepers are widely used by professional mechanics but, being mounted on castors, they tend to shoot out from under you just as you are pulling hardest on some obstinate bolt. For this reason I use a cheaper and more comfortable alternative of a wooden lid from an engine packing case with some thick polystyrene laid on it, covered by an old blanket or a piece of carpet. If you are working right underneath, a hard cushion used as a pillow will take a lot of strain off your neck.

Good lighting is essential to avoid damaging the car or injuring yourself, but mains-voltage inspection lamps can

be very dangerous, especially if the bulb breaks and exposes the live filament. A low-voltage lamp operating through a mains transformer is much safer, and 24-volt 'rough service' bulbs withstand the rigours of workshop use better than ordinary mains bulbs. Alternatively 24-volt fluorescent lamps, which can be manoeuvred into all sorts of awkward places by virtue of their slimness, are also available.

Fig. 1:1. Even if you are adept with a hammer and can split a joint like a professional, a ball-joint splitter is pretty well a necessity

You will also need some protective clothing, and you cannot beat a good *cotton* boiler suit (the nylon variety is easily damaged by anything hot). Bib-and-brace overalls leave your arms and much of your chest unprotected, whilst lab or warehouse coats do the same for your legs— their tails also flap about, so that when you want their protection it isn't there. As a great deal of dirt can fall from the car, a pair of clear goggles to protect your eyes is an excellent idea, together with a hat of some sort to keep your hair clean. Working in trainers or other lightweight shoes is not advisable—wear stout leather shoes or boots, ideally Toetectors or one of the other metal-reinforced types.

Dismantling the car's underpinnings can be made much more pleasant by some prior cleaning. Steam cleaning is ideal, and if you cannot get your car to the cleaner, he may have a mobile unit that he can bring to you. Failing that,

Fig. 1:2. For lightweight wire wheels, such as on this pre-war Austin Seven, you will need a spoke nipple key to keep the spokes tight and the wheel running true. Note the unusual quarter-elliptic cantilever road spring

one of the much advertised high-pressure water cleaners might be a good alternative. If you are on a tight budget, you will be surprised at how effective a determined onslaught with a wire brush, paraffin (*not* petrol), rag, scrubbing brush and hot water can be.

Springs capable of supporting the car when loaded contain a lot of latent energy—enough to cause serious injury—and coil springs must *always* be restrained before being removed. In many cases you will need special clamps or compressors, so that you can release their energy gradually and safely. Don't improvise. The final cost could be very high!

The equipment used in garages for checking steering and suspension geometry is often sophisticated and almost always expensive. Its purchase by the amateur, therefore, is not likely to be worthwhile unless it can be bought cheaply at a closing-down auction or from a dealer in second-hand garage equipment. On the other hand, if the restoration project is not suffering from serious accident damage, and if it is taken to pieces very carefully, making marks or taking measurements so that everything goes back into its original position, it is unlikely that there will be many problems when a check is made by a garage on completion of the work.

Like steering geometry apparatus, a wheel balancer does not come cheaply, with the possible exception of the 'EasO Bal' which was inexpensive and fairly effective. One of these might prove useful if it can be bought second-hand. Whilst on the subject of wheels, a very inexpensive item is the spoke nipple key which will be of considerable help in prolonging the life of wire-spoke wheels (unless they are on a Ford where the spokes are welded in). Add to this a spoke die, if you can find one, and a stock of unthreaded spokes of the right gauge and you will extend your ability to restore and look after wire wheels.

If your vehicle is one of the very many older Fords with curved, transverse springs, you ought to try to find one of the curved-spring spreaders specially made for these cars (or make one instead—see chapter 7). Otherwise you will be in for a lot of sweating and, if you're that kind of person, swearing!

As with so many other automotive jobs, an oxy-acetylene welding kit has many uses when working on the suspension or steering: loosening tight bolts, moving 'immovable' king pins, burning out old composite rubber and metal bushes (take care not to inhale the smoke—your paint-spraying mask will protect you), and replacing rust-rotted pivots or anchorages with home-fabricated replacements.

Tyre levers are useful for much more than just fitting and removing tyres. Two or three big ones and a pry bar are very helpful in moving all sorts of things and in detecting suspension wear by lifting and levering sideways.

I like to dislodge steering ball joints by using two substantial hammers: a club hammer of, say, 4 lb (2 kg) as a support and a $1\frac{1}{2}$–2 lb (0.75–1 kg) hammer to hit the

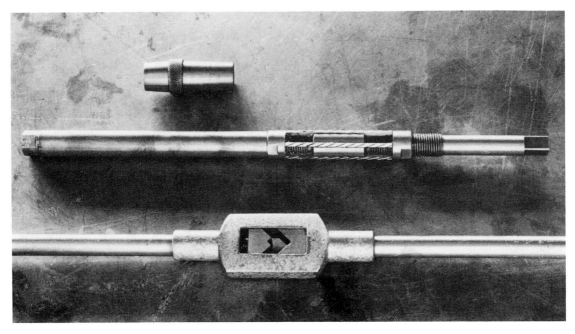

Fig. 1:3. An adjustable reamer is an essential tool when replacing king-pin bushes on a beam axle

steering arm. If you doubt your ability in using hammers (a missed blow can cause a lot of damage to threads or dirt excluders) or there is not enough room to swing one, you will need a ball-joint splitter.

Many cars built by British Leyland towards the end of what is now referred to as the 'classic' period used 'Hydrolastic' or 'Hydragas' suspensions. As the cars become obsolete and increasing numbers of Leyland garages move over to other franchises, there may be an opportunity to buy one of the pressurizing units for these suspensions at a bargain price. If you are restoring a car with this type of suspension, it would be foolish not to grab the chance.

Your restoration project may employ king pins as steering pivots. When these and their bushes need renewing, the latter must be reamed to size. Since this job will almost certainly need doing as part of the restoration, it is a good idea to buy a suitable reamer. Choose either the ordinary piloted, adjustable reamer which is used with parallel king pins, or the non-adjustable, stepped reamer which is needed for cars such as the 'Farina' range made by

BMC (latterly BMH and BL). You will probably recoup the cost of the reamer the first time you use it. However, reamers are precision tools and must be looked after. Mine is wrapped in 'Ban Rust' paper and kept in its original box in a warm fireside-cupboard indoors.

Large nuts of more than 1 in. (25 mm) across the flats are common in steering and suspension systems. As well as being very tight they are likely to be very difficult to obtain, so you will need the appropriate sockets to be able to deal with them without fear of personal injury and without resorting to 'butchery'. Take care to see that they are the right size, bearing in mind that they may be made to the Whitworth, Unified or Metric systems. If you can afford them, heavy-duty $\frac{3}{4}$ in. drive sockets are likely to be more 'persuasive' than their $\frac{1}{2}$ in. counterparts, but both will be more effective on really tight nuts if supplemented by some heat from the welding kit.

Quite a lot has been said here about personal safety. Remember that as well as having a lot to do with your enjoyment of the restored car, the standards to which you work, in terms of what you decide to do and how you execute the work, will affect your safety and that of others. This must be kept in mind constantly and bear on every decision you make when restoring the steering and suspension systems.

Chapter 2 | Basics of steering

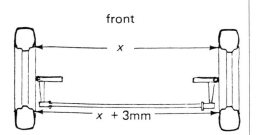

front

Fig. 2:1. Toe in is the difference between x and x + y, y in this case being 3 mm (courtesy of Hutchinson Education)

This is a practical book. It is not intended to go into vehicle behaviour and handling in depth, but some knowledge of the angles which comprise the steering and suspension geometry and of the way the vehicle moves on its tyres can be invaluable in finding the causes of steering faults. It may also prevent the home mechanic making silly errors and suggest in terms of, say, something as simple as tyre pressures, ways of improving the car's behaviour.

Front wheel alignment

The best known of the angles and the one to which the ordinary car user almost always attributes steering or tyre-wear faults is the 'toe-in setting' or 'tracking', perhaps more accurately 'front wheel alignment'.

On a rear-wheel-drive car the distance between the front wheel rims is set so that it is slightly less in front of the wheel centres than it is behind them. Thus both front wheels point inwards slightly, a condition known as 'toe in'. The reason for this is that when the car moves forwards, the wheels oppose that movement initially, causing the stub axles to turn outwards slightly on the steering swivels. (This is because of the slight play present in the steering and suspension joints.) If the wheels were perfectly parallel when the car was stationary they would both point outwards when it was moving forwards, which would cause the car to wander. Setting the wheels to toe in at rest means that they will adopt a parallel position when on the move, helping to maintain straight-line stability.

On a front-wheel-drive car the situation is reversed; the turning force applied to the front wheels by the drive shafts tends to push them inwards when the car is driven

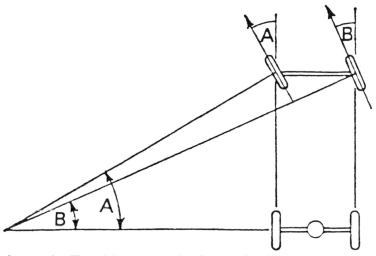

forwards. For this reason the front wheels are sometimes set to 'toe out' at rest—the rims being further apart ahead of the wheel centres than behind them so that they swing parallel under drive. In other instances, this effect is obtained by different means.

Fig. 2:2. Inner wheel A has to be turned more than wheel B to negotiate a turn (courtesy of Hutchinson Education)

Toe out on turns

When a car rounds a bend, the inside front wheel needs to be turned at a greater angle (given more lock) than that on the outside. This is because the wheels follow parallel arcs, the outer arc being of a greater radius than the inner one. Therefore they must be made to 'toe out on turns', and this is arranged by having an Ackermann steering linkage. Under this system, imaginary lines projected through the steering-swivel centres and steering-arm joints (when viewed from above) meet at a point on the car's centre line about 2–3 ft (0.6–0.9 m) ahead of the rear axle. When correctly set, the system will ensure that when making a turn and the outer wheel is at an angle of 20 degrees, the inner wheel will be at about 22 degrees. Toe out on turns is related directly to the toe-in setting (or steering alignment), and if this is not set correctly there may be a tendency for the car to turn more easily in one direction than the other. It may also produce rapid and uneven tyre wear.

If the car has a beam front axle the steering arms will be

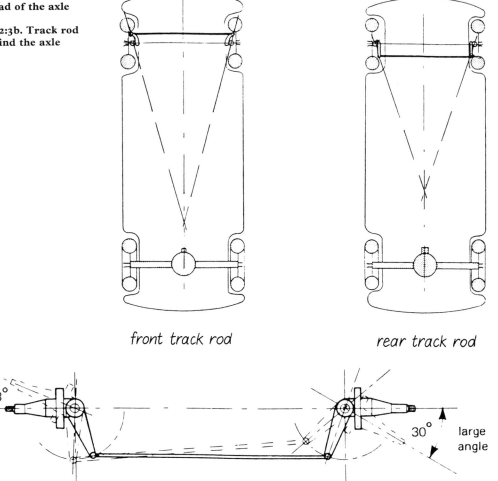

Right **Fig. 2:3a. Track rod mounted ahead of the axle**

Far right **Fig. 2:3b. Track rod mounted behind the axle**

front track rod   *rear track rod*

small angle 23°

30° large angle

Fig. 2:3c. Steering-arm inclination produces toe out on turns (Figs. 2:3a/b/c courtesy of Hutchinson Education)

joined by a simple link called a track rod which will have a threaded joint at each end. The purpose of the threaded joints is to provide toe-in setting adjustment by allowing the length of the track rod to be altered. Normally the nearside joint has a left-hand thread and the offside joint a right-hand thread so that adjustments can be made without having to disconnect the track rod from the steering arms. This system is foolproof since any alteration of track-rod length automatically provides an equal amount of toe out on turns in both directions. When the toe-in setting is

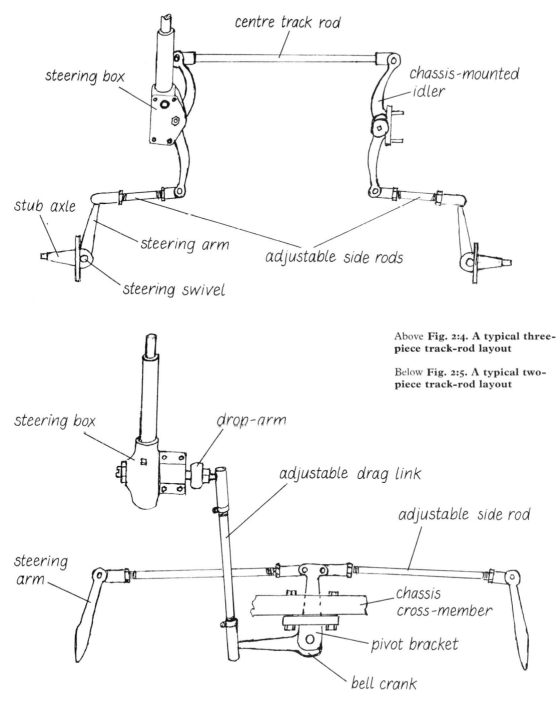

centre track rod

steering box

chassis-mounted idler

stub axle

steering arm

adjustable side rods

steering swivel

Above **Fig. 2:4. A typical three-piece track-rod layout**

Below **Fig. 2:5. A typical two-piece track-rod layout**

steering box

drop-arm

adjustable drag link

adjustable side rod

steering arm

chassis cross-member

pivot bracket

bell crank

correct, toe out on turns will also be correct.

Where a car has independent front suspension (ifs) the connection between the steering arms is normally by a two- or three-piece track-rod system. Typical two-piece systems are the rack-and-pinion design used on the Riley RM series and the lever arrangement on the VW Beetle and the Aston Martin DB 2/4. Three-piece systems come in two basic forms. One has a long, centre track rod (usually of fixed length) between the steering box and an idler on the other side of the car, with a short, adjustable track rod at each end. This can be seen on the Rootes Alpine/Rapier/Gazelle/Minx series. A few cars, such as the A30/A35, have an adjustable centre rod with short, fixed track rods at the ends. The other three-piece system has a rack-and-pinion unit in the middle with a short, adjustable track rod at each end. The Morris Minor is a well-known employer of this system. The important point to remember with these systems is that *if the short, adjustable track rods are not adjusted by equal amounts, toe out on turns will be incorrect.*

This must always be borne in mind when adjusting the track. Toe out on turns can only be measured on turntable plates which the amateur restorer is unlikely to possess. Therefore, you will have to take the car to a garage. If the toe out on turns is incorrect but the length of the track rods is equal, a steering arm is probably bent or loose.

Camber

The wheels are provided with camber to reduce steering effort and the bending load applied to the stub axle. It also helps provide 'straight-ahead stability' and keep the linkage taut. If the wheel leans outwards when viewed from the front, it has 'positive' camber; if it leans in, it has 'negative' camber. The camber angle is measured between the plane of the wheel and true vertical.

In most cases the front wheels are set with positive camber, the purpose being to arrange the centre line of the wheel and tyre to intersect the centre line of the king pin or steering swivels near ground level. In this way when the wheel is turned it pivots about a fixed point rather than being dragged round in an arc. Not only does this make

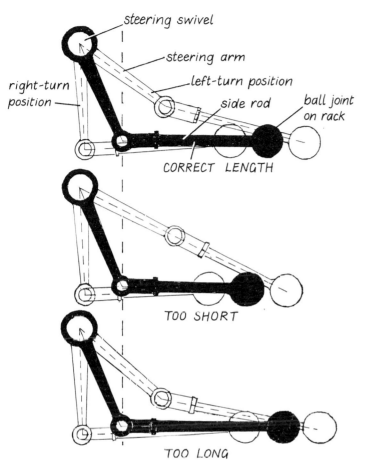

Above left **Fig. 2:6. Unequal side-rod settings affect the toe out on turns, i.e. it is not enough merely to set the toe in**

Above **Fig. 2:7. The Hillman Imp had pronounced positive camber**

steering less of an effort, but it also reduces tyre wear. If the camber angle on one side of the car is greater than that on the other, the car will 'pull' towards the side having the larger positive camber (or smaller negative camber).

Whilst cars with beam axles generally have a fairly large positive camber angle (3–7 degrees), those with independent suspension have smaller positive angles or sometimes a negative angle. You can calculate the camber angle yourself, but in practice it makes more sense to take the car to a garage and have it measured. It is possible to adjust the camber on some post-war cars with ifs. On the Rootes Alpine/Rapier/Gazelle/Minx it is done by adding or removing shims at the inner pivot attachment of the upper wishbone; a similar arrangement is used on Jaguar Mk I and Mk II saloons. Lea Francis cars had an eccentric adjuster on the outer spindle of the upper wishbone. However, in most cases the camber is non-adjustable and if it is outside the specified limits some parts, or the structure of the car itself, are damaged.

Castor

As the name implies, this is a similar arrangement to that found on a furniture castor and refers to the angle between the king pin or steering-swivel axis and the vertical when viewed from the side (Fig. 2:11). The projected axis of the steering swivel meets the road ahead of the tyre 'contact patch', its purpose being to assist straight-line stability by providing a 'self-centring' action to the front wheels. When the wheels are turned, the tyre contact patches move to one side of the axis and, unless they are held there by the steering wheel, the forward motion of the car will tend to force them back in line. The greater the castor angle, the stronger the self-centring action. The distance between the point where the steering-swivel axis meets the ground and the centre of the tyre contact patch is sometimes referred to as the 'trail'.

Like camber, castor is rarely adjustable. However, it can be altered with shims on Mk I and Mk II Jaguars, and by a screwed spindle on the E type. Incorrect castor on a car with ifs generally means something is damaged, but if the car has a beam axle the castor angle reduces as the leaf springs flatten or settle with age. If you cannot have the springs reset immediately, fitting a steel wedge between the spring and the axle will improve the car's straight-line stability.

Steering-swivel inclination

This used to be called king pin inclination (KPI) and refers to the angle made between the king pin or steering-swivel axis and the vertical when viewed from the front of the car.

Very early in the development of steering systems it was believed that by making the steering-swivel centre line intersect the plane of the wheel at ground level, very 'light' steering could be provided. This was true, but the result

Top left **Fig. 2:8. Positive camber on some cars, for example the Sunbeam Alpine shown, could be increased by the removal of shims at the upper-wishbone mounting**

Top right **Fig. 2:9. The castor effect**

Bottom left **Fig. 2:10. By drawing one line through the cycle steering head and another vertically through the spindle, one can see how trail is measured**

Bottom right **Fig. 2:11. The same theory applied to the automobile**

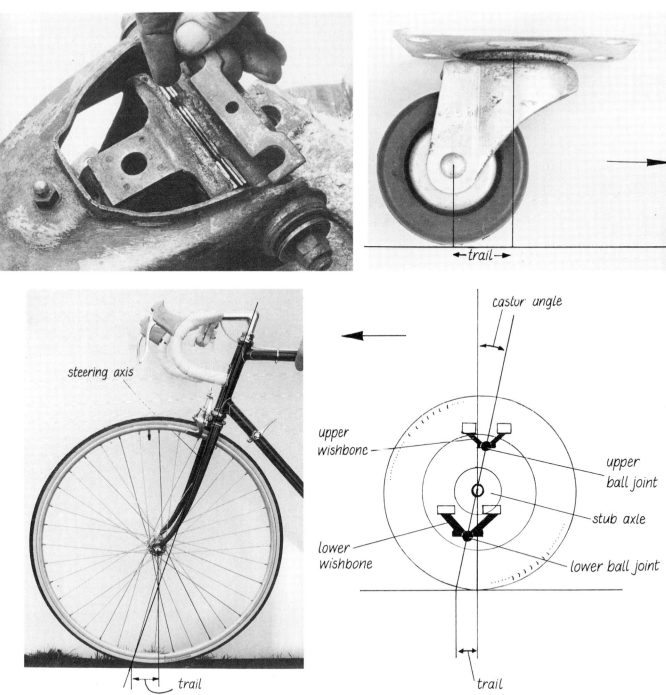

trail

steering axis

trail

castor angle

upper
wishbone

upper
ball joint

stub axle

lower
wishbone

lower ball joint

trail

was oversensitive, 'twitchy' steering. As a result, the point of intersection was moved below ground level, giving a 'positive offset' between the centre of the tyre contact patch and the point where the steering-swivel axis met the ground. This had a damping effect on the steering (Fig. 2:13). In more recent times, in an effort to reduce the dramatic and dangerous effects of a front tyre bursting at speed, a new concept of 'negative offset' was introduced.

Previously, when a front tyre burst, the steering tended to snatch towards the deflated tyre because of the increased drag it caused in contact with the road and because distortion of the tyre moved the centre of its contact patch outwards, increasing positive offset and providing a high degree of leverage away from the direction of travel. When negative offset is employed (Fig. 2:14), the steering-swivel axis is inclined at quite a large angle, perhaps as much as 15 degrees to the vertical, so that it intersects the plane of the wheel *above* ground level and meets the road *outside* the tyre centre line. If a tyre is deflated suddenly, the outward movement of the contact-patch centre tends to reduce the offset rather than increase it, improving stability in this condition.

Fig. 2:12. Imaginary lines through the centre of the wheel and the king pin intersect at ground level

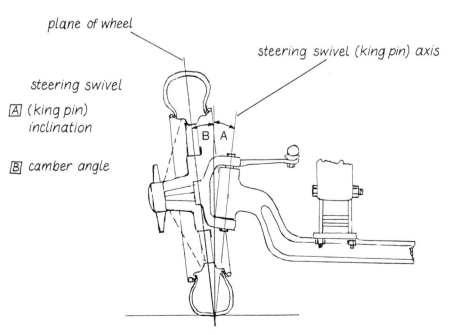

plane of wheel

steering swivel (king pin) axis

steering swivel

A (king pin) inclination

B camber angle

B A

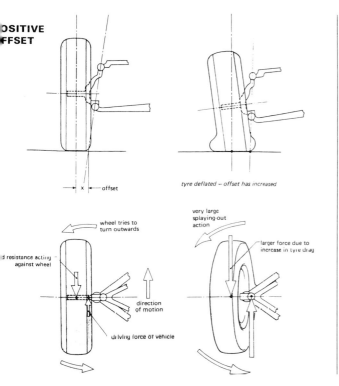

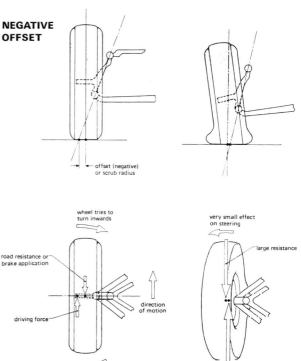

Oversteer and understeer

When a vehicle is moving in a curved path, centrifugal effects create a side force that acts against it. A side force can also be created by the wind or by gravity on a cambered road. Any side force will create understeering/oversteering conditions.

Because the tyres are made of flexible rubber they deflect under the action of the side force, the amount of deflection depending on the amount of force applied, the tyre pressure, the tyre construction (radial or cross-ply) and the weight supported by the tyres. If both front and rear tyres are deflected by the same amount, the car would simply drift away sideways from the force. If, however, the deflection of the front tyres was greater than that of the rear, the car would *turn away* from the force (understeer). If the deflection of the rear tyres was greater than that of the front tyres, the car would *turn towards* the force (oversteer). The angle between the steered path of the

Above left **Fig. 2:13. Traditional positive wheel offset**

Above **Fig. 2:14. Modern negative offset facilitates fail-safe steering (Figs. 2:13/14 courtesy of Hutchinson Education)**

Right **Fig. 2:15. When a side force is applied to a wheel it induces a deflection in the tyre termed its slip angle (courtesy of Hutchinson Education)**

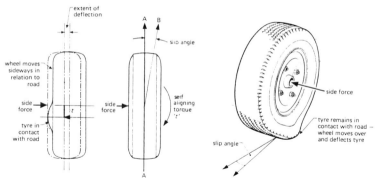

Below **Fig. 2:16. Cross-ply tyres had both their rim width and their diameter marked in inches**

wheel and its actual path over the road is called the 'slip angle' (although in reality no slip occurs). When a car understeers, the slip angle of the front wheels is greater than that of the rear, and vice versa.

Therefore an understeering car tends to run wide on corners, turn away from a side wind or run down a camber, and holding it against these forces is a fairly natural reaction. An oversteering car tends to tuck into a corner, turn towards a side wind or run up a camber—unnatural actions which most drivers find difficult to cope with.

Often oversteer is countered by a big difference in pressures between the front and rear tyres. In the Hillman Imp, for example, the front-tyre pressure was *half* of that of the rear! It is also common for rear-engined cars to have large positive camber and castor angles to assist in preventing oversteer.

If a car is fitted with radial tyres at the front and cross-plies at the rear, the result is violent oversteer. For this reason, such a combination is *illegal*.

Above **Fig. 2:17. On radial tyres the rim width is in millimetres and the wheel diameter is in inches. The letters SR and S are speed ratings, explained in chapter 11, whilst the number 86 is a load rating, in this case 530 kg maximum**

Right **Fig. 2:18. Diagramatically this is what is meant by understeer and oversteer (courtesy of Hutchinson Education)**

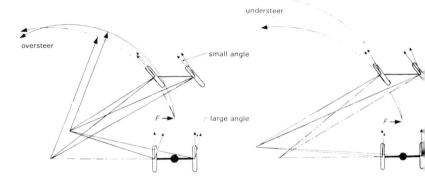

Chapter 3 | Assessing steering/front suspension condition

Fig. 3:1. To test the steering-column top bush, rock the steering wheel back and forth

A good place to begin evaluating a car's steering and suspension is in the driver's seat, but not while driving. The steering wheel and column are often overlooked by the amateur mechanic looking for steering faults or when preparing the car for its annual Department of Transport (MOT) test.

Start by pushing and pulling the wheel in and out, and up and down, looking for insecure column mountings at the bulkhead and dashboard and for wear in the steering-column top bush. The latter is quite common but the bush is often an easily replaced felt item. By rocking the wheel make sure that it is tight on the steering-shaft splines or taper. Also check that the wheel is correctly positioned when the road wheels are pointing straight ahead.

By pushing and pulling along the length of the column you will be able to detect wear or slackness in any flexible or universal joints and, on cars fitted with rack-and-pinion steering, whether there is any movement at the clamp attaching the steering shaft to the steering pinion. This test will also reveal excess end-play in a steering box.

Rock the steering wheel gently to and fro, assessing the free-play in the system. It is difficult to specify what is reasonable. However, if steering is by rack-and-pinion, much less play is permissible than where a steering box is used—as a very approximate guide, about $\frac{1}{2}$ in. (13 mm) measured at the wheel rim for rack-and-pinion steering and not more than 3 in. (75 mm) for a steering box. Check that the steering wheel rim and its spokes are not cracked or broken.

Next it is necessary to get under the car to watch the

Fig. 3:2. By turning the steering wheel from left to right one can check the free-play

action of the steering mechanism with the weight of the vehicle supported on its wheels. You do need space to inspect it. A lift or a pit would be ideal, but if you have neither, a pair of ramps will suffice if they are sited on a firm, level base. Get someone to sit in the driver's seat and rock the wheel firmly, but not violently, to and fro while you look at all of the moving parts.

This test can show up all sorts of defects. Steering boxes or idlers may exhibit worn bushes or vertical free-play (a little is permissible), or their attachment bolts might be loose, the chassis/body mounting might be cracked, or the drop-arm/steering lever might not be tight on its shaft. Ball-pin joints in the linkage may show wear or have split dirt-excluder rubbers, or they may not be tightened fully into their tapers.

Although an uncommon fault, it is possible for a steering arm to be loose at its attachment to the stub axle. Such a fault is very dangerous, and it is usual for steering arms to be held by self-locking or split-pinned nuts for security. Take a good look while you are there to make sure that no drop-arm, relay lever, steering arm or any part of the linkage is bent.

Whilst on the subject of damage, look for any rippling of the chassis around the steering box, idler or rack-and-pinion unit as a result of any previous accident. Often such ripples will eventually split. The only satisfactory repair is likely to be new chassis legs.

Many steering columns incorporate a universal joint or, sometimes, a flexible coupling. These, too, must be subjected to the rocking check. They should also be checked while the steering is being turned from lock to lock with the wheels clear of the ground and the weight of the car on the suspension so that it is compressed to its normal ride height. At the same time make sure that no part of the steering or suspension linkage fouls a brake pipe.

If the car has power-assisted steering, check that the pump drive belt is tight, that the pump turns and that its mountings are secure. Make sure there are no fluid leaks and that power assistance is given.

The next set of checks concern the wheel bearings. As you jack up the car to check the wheel bearings keep a close

eye on the stub axle, its king pin or swivels and its suspension linkages. Look especially for any slack movement as the weight is transferred from the wheel to the jack. What you might expect to find, if the car has a king-pin type of steering swivel, is excessive vertical free-play due to a worn thrust washer or bearing. If screwed swivels are employed there might be some movement at the trunnions indicating wear. A badly worn bush might also show up in rubber-bushed steering linkages. Remember that the suspension will move considerably as the car is raised. What you are looking for is abnormal movement due to wear. Remember, too, that so far as the suspension is concerned this is a preliminary check to be followed by a more detailed examination later.

With the car supported safely, spin each wheel while listening for any noise denoting roughness and feeling for any tightness indicating a badly worn bearing. Stop the wheel, grasp it at top and bottom and rock it in a vertical plane. Slack in the wheel bearings will be shown up by movement of the drum or disc relative to the stub axle. If the stub axle moves, the slack is in the steering swivels. If these are king pins the wear can normally be seen clearly. Front-wheel bearings comprising angular-contact ball

Above left **Fig. 3:3. The arrows to this steering box show: a) steering column end-play; b) rocker shaft end-play; c) rocker shaft radial-play which is due to either a worn shaft or worn bushes**

Above **Fig. 3:4. Steering arms, such as this Morris Minor one, should be closely examined for damage**

Above **Fig. 3:5. Flexible steering-column joints, such as found on the Triumph Spitfire, must be checked for wear and disintegration**

Top right **Fig. 3:6. Power-steering belts, as on this Rover V8, should be checked for wear and adjustment**

Centre right **Fig. 3:7. On cars with beam axles, like this 1930s Morris Ten, check for vertical movement of the stub axle which will indicate wear in the bearings or thrust washers**

Bottom right **Fig. 3:8. Constant-velocity joint gaiters should never be cracked or split and always make sure the retaining clip is in place (courtesy of Austin Rover Ltd)** races or taper rollers will be adjustable to reduce free-play, but remember taper-roller wheel bearings normally require just a little play, for example, $\frac{1}{16}$ in. (1.5 mm), at the wheel rim for correct adjustment. In the absence of any other guidance, from a workshop manual or whatever, tighten the retaining nut until you *just* feel resistance and then slacken the nut until the locking split pin can be fitted.

On a front-wheel-drive car you will not be able to spin the wheel by hand very easily, but it should still turn. While doing so, look closely at the gaiters which protect the universal joints, making sure they are not split and that their securing clips are in place. Check that the universal joints turn smoothly without any clicking or grinding noises as the wheels are turned from lock to lock, and that the drive shafts are not bent. Evidence of the impending failure of a constant-velocity (CV) universal joint can sometimes be obtained by trying to drive the car away from rest against the brakes, first forwards and then backwards, while listening for clicking sounds. Also try driving in a low gear in tight (full-lock) circles to left and right, with some pressure on the brake pedal and a fairly wide throttle opening. Listen for harsh grinding or rumbling noises from the joint on the *inside* of the turn.

Steering and suspension are closely related, and the following checks cover items of both. In every case the vehicle must be lifted, but the point at which it is jacked and the method employed for testing will depend on the type of suspension fitted. If it has a beam axle or ifs combining a coil spring and wishbones, jack the car so that the spring is loaded and grasp the wheel at top and bottom, preferably with your upper hand just behind the vertical centre line of the wheel and your lower hand just in front of it. Try to rock the wheel while looking for movement between the king pins and their bushes, and if the car has ifs, between the wishbone pins and their pivots. Movement in excess of about $\frac{1}{16}$ in. (1.5 mm), in addition to any slack attributable to the wheel bearings, will require rectification.

If you have a front-wheel-drive car with the suspension layout shown in Fig. 3:10 (3/3a), the jack must be placed beneath the vehicle's structure (often a subframe) near the

Fig. 3:9. To ascertain steering-swivel or wheel-bearing wear, rock the wheel from top to bottom

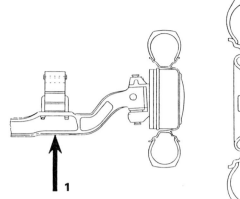

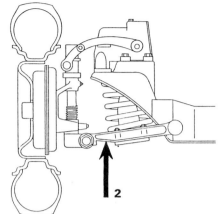

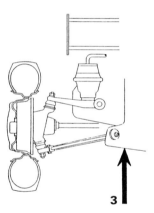

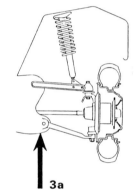

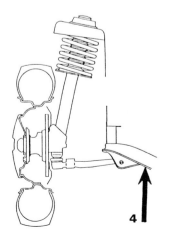

Fig. 3:10. This diagram shows recommended jacking points for cars with: 1) beam axle; 2) coil spring and double wishbone; 3) fwd car with rubber or rubber-hydraulic suspension; 3a) fwd car with coil-spring suspension; 4) MacPherson strut suspension (courtesy of Controller of Her Majesty's Stationery Office)

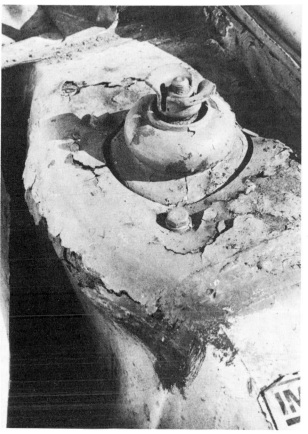

lower inner pivot of the suspension. Grasping the wheel as before, shake it violently in a vertical plane while looking for movement at the ball swivels.

On MacPherson strut suspension, you will be looking for wear between the strut and its damper/oil reservoir, at the track-control arm and at the upper support bearing. You should also look for fluid leakage from the damper unit, excess wear between the damper unit and the strut, and for badly corroded top plates where the upper support bearing is attached to the body. Jack the car adjacent to the inner pivot of the track-control arm—Fig. 3:10 (4). When the wheel is clear of the ground, it should be shaken violently in its vertical and fore-and-aft planes while looking for wear. Have someone turn the steering wheel

Above left **Fig. 3:11. Ford Mk II Consuls and other cars with these early MacPherson struts should be checked for: a) leakage around the gland seal; b) ball-joint or bush wear on the track-control arm**

Above **Fig. 3:12. MacPherson strut mountings are prone to rust as you can see on this Escort**

Fig. 3:13. More rust, this time near the bottom suspension-arm pivot of a Morris Minor, seriously affecting the performance of steering and suspension, and ultimately safety

gently from lock to lock as you listen for sounds of a worn top bearing. Look for signs of perishing or separation of the rubber bush (if there is one) surrounding the top bearing.

When inspecting the steering and suspension always look very carefully for rust in structural members within 1 ft (300 mm) of any mounting. Well-known trouble spots are the aforementioned upper-bearing mounting plates on Fords with MacPherson strut suspension, and around the inner pivot of the lower suspension arm on the Morris Minor and its close relatives, the Wolseley 1500 and Riley 1.5.

Should you decide to repair the damage by welding, it is *essential* that the work is done thoroughly with material of adequate gauge. If, as on the Minor, an eye bolt passes through a chassis leg it is vital to include a strengthening tube of adequate section through which the pivot bolt fits. The repair section needed is fairly simple in shape and within the scope of most enthusiasts to make, but if you are in any doubt use a pre-manufactured item. If you are a novice welder and unsure of the quality of your welds, leave this important work to someone with more expertise. When fitting a repair plate to a Ford or similar car with MacPherson strut suspension, make sure that the repair section is large enough to reach back to some really sound

metal and cut away the 'diseased' areas completely.

Your car may have steel or rubber springs, the latter possibly supplemented by hydraulics (as in a Hydrolastic system), or it may have hydro-pneumatic suspension with a combination of hydraulics and compressed gas providing both springing and damping (for example, Hydragas).

Steel springs may be semi-elliptic leaves, coils or torsion bars. The last seldom give any trouble at all. If there is any settling of the bar an adjustment can be made on most cars to take account of this, usually by slackening a lock nut and tightening an adjusting screw. It should be noted that new torsion bars may be fitted to either side of the car. However, once fitted a torsion bar must *always* be kept to the same side. Remember, too, the potentially dangerous pent-up energy it contains. Never attempt to put an identifying or aligning mark on a torsion bar using a dot punch, chisel or letter/number stamp; use typists' correction fluid instead.

Coil springs settle and occasionally break, as do the leaves of semi-elliptics—usually the main one. To test the bushes and shackles of a leaf spring try to move the spring vertically on its shackle pins and rock it sideways on its shackles by levering against the chassis with a pry bar or tyre lever. (This can be seen in the photographs above.)

Above left **Fig. 3:14. A tyre lever can be used to test leaf-spring shackles for wear**

Above **Fig. 3:15. A pry bar is used on this Morris Minor to test for sideways movement in the leaf-spring shackle**

Rubber springs last well but they should be inspected for obvious damage such as splitting. If your car has one of the hydraulic-based systems, such as Hydrolastic or Hydragas, walk round the car to see if it appears to have 'sunk' on its suspension. As a check, measure vertically from the centre of each wheel to the top of the wheel arch and compare the measurements with those quoted in the manual or, at least, from side to side. If there is any difference, check the displacer unit at each wheel and the connecting pipework for hydraulic fluid leaks.

Dampers are generally and inaccurately referred to as 'shock absorbers'. They don't absorb shocks, their function being to prevent the continuing oscillation of the springs. They are not normally repairable and may fail in three ways:

1. They may no longer perform their damping function, due to an internal fault, and produce a very bouncy ride.
2. They may suffer a fluid leak.
3. They may become very stiff or seize completely, producing a very hard, rough ride.

An 'MOT' tester has to assess dampers without taking them off the car or even disconnecting them. He does this

Below **Fig. 3:16. Testing a lever-arm damper**

Below right **Fig. 3:17. Testing a telescopic damper**

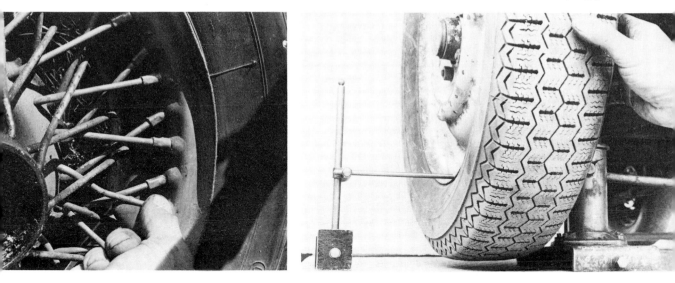

by bouncing the car—when it is well under way he stops; the car's body should stop moving within one oscillation. The car restorer is in a less restricted situation and would be well advised to remove the dampers to inspect them. The telescopic, lever or vane types of damper should be moved through their entire range of travel, and there should be a constant resistance to movement in both directions (but not necessarily the same level of resistance). A damper that has a jerky movement, is partially seized or is leaking, must be rejected. The bushes and the eyes into which they are fitted must also be in sound condition.

When assessing the steering and suspension, you should spend some time on the wheels and tyres. Pressed-steel wheels are remarkably trouble free and are unlikely to be in poor condition, except as the result of kerbing or other accidental damage, or as the result of clumsy tyre fitting. Wire wheels should be examined for loose or broken spokes. Tyres should be concentric with the rim, free from perishing, cuts, cracks or bulges, and have a minimum tread depth of 1 mm all over. If two of the tyres are radials and two cross-plies, the radials must be at the rear.

Above left **Fig. 3:18. Wire-wheel spokes can easily be damaged by careless use of the copper clouter hammer**

Above **Fig. 3:19. The run-out on a wheel should not exceed 0.125 in. (3 mm) in either plane**

Chapter 4 | Steering overhaul

Fig. 4:1. Two hammers are used in the professional method of cracking the taper on a ball joint

All steering systems use linkages with ball joints; earlier cars had joints which were grease-lubricated, but later on sealed units, pre-lubricated on assembly, came into use. These have a long life before replacement is necessary, but the life of the earlier type depends on the frequency and thoroughness with which the regular lubrication has been done.

One of the jobs which often proves daunting to the amateur mechanic is that of separating the ball-joint tapers from the steering arms, drop-arms and relay levers. The traditional way is to use two hammers: a heavy one to support the arm near its tapered hole, and another lighter one to hit it and shock the tapers free. You do need to be able to wield a hammer effectively to do this and you also need space in which to swing it. If there is no room for a supporting hammer on one side while you hit the other, an endways blow along the length of the arm or lever often does the trick.

If you are not as proficient with a hammer as you would like to be or if there is insufficient space to swing one, a screw-operated ball-joint splitter is required. There are two types—one acting on a wedging principle and the other by levering. Of the two, I prefer the latter. Whatever method you choose for splitting the joint, it is a good idea to protect the end of the threaded pin by replacing the locking nut and adjusting it until it is just flush with the top of the pin. If the joint is to be reused you must be careful not to damage its rubber boot, which keeps out water and dirt and retains the grease. If it is split or its garter spring is damaged, rapid wear will result.

With the ball joints separated and the links on the bench,

you can slacken the clamp bolts, or lock nuts, and unscrew the joints from the tubes or rods. *Don't* do this until you have some record of the distance between the two joints on that particular link. Before taking the joints off, centralize the tapered, threaded stud of each, lay the link on the garage floor and mark the centre line of each joint on it as a guide for reassembly. If, as is often the case, the joints do not lie in the same plane, make a simple pencil sketch to show their relative positions. All of this will help reduce the hassle when you come to put it all back together again.

Where a single track rod is used, as on nearly every car with a beam axle, the rod will almost certainly have right- and left-hand threads at opposite ends. Remember this when you undo the joints. On replacing the rod, fit the left-hand threaded end to the left-hand steering arm. Where twin track rods are used, they must be adjusted so that their lengths are equal.

Cars which have a beam axle have a drag link to connect the steering box to the rest of the linkage. The length of the drag link affects the centralizing of the steering wheel spokes when the vehicle is moving in a straight line, so be sure this measurement is correct also. The drag-link ball joints are often at 90 degrees to each other—bear in mind the point made earlier. Do not use the drag link to alter the steering wheel position without first making sure that the wheel itself is in its correct position on the shaft, and the drop-arm is also in its right place on the steering-box output shaft. These positions are often fixed by the wheel

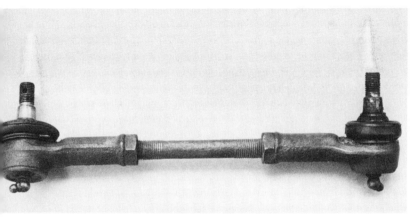

Fig. 4:2. Chalk marks can be used as an approximate measure of length when replacing side-rod ends

or arm being keyed in place, but they may be splined, in which case some sort of alignment mark is often provided in the form of a chisel or dot-punch mark.

After replacing the ball joints at the track-rod ends, it is necessary to check the front wheel alignment (see chapter 2).

Steering swivels

There are four distinct types of steering swivel:

1. King pins—the oldest method. The pin is usually clamped in the axle beam or, in the case of independent suspension, held between the ends of the suspension arms. The stub axle carrying the road wheel pivots about the pin on phosphor-bronze, or sometimes brass, bushes.
2. Screwed swivels. Usually the swivel proper has male threads at each end which screw into female-threaded trunnions carried by the upper and lower suspension arms. The Morris Minor is one of the best-known cars with this system.
3. Ball joints. As these are spherical they allow movement in all directions to accommodate steering and suspension movement.
4. Suspension dampers, which also act as steering swivels—generally referred to as MacPherson struts.

Renewing king pins and bushes

Where a beam axle is fitted to the car, it may be possible to replace the king pins and their bushes without removing it. However, the work will be easier if the axle is taken off, although it may take a bit longer. If the repair is part of a restoration rather than just a necessary job, you will want to check that the axle is not bent and to paint it. In either case, you will have to disconnect the steering linkage (as described above), remove the road wheels, their bearings and the brake back plates. If the car has hydraulic brakes you might be able to avoid the tedious business of bleeding them by tying the back plates to some other part of the car so that the pipes are not kinked or strained. Much the same goes for cable brakes, but rod-operated versions must be disconnected at the nearest convenient yoke and clevis joint. You will also need to disconnect the dampers, if any.

To remove the axle, the car must be lifted and supported beneath its frame so that the axle hangs on the springs. Take the weight of the axle on a trolley jack, undo the 'U' bolts holding the axle to the springs and lower it to the ground.

Wipe any grease from the stub axles and scrape, wipe or wire-brush away the road dirt from the axle. The next move is to release the cotter pins securing the king pins to the axle beam. These can be quite obstinate and a good anvil will be a great help. Unscrew each cotter-pin nut until it is flush with the end of the pin's thread, then support the axle on the anvil using a thick piece of steel tube of about $\frac{1}{2}$ in. (13 mm) bore and $1\frac{1}{2}$ in. (37 mm) long to surround the unthreaded end of the cotter pin. A hefty whack on the threaded end, using a 2 lb (1 kg) hammer and a piece of $\frac{3}{4}$ in. (18 mm) steel rod as a punch, will usually free the pin. If it does not, some heat may help persuade it to move. This is best applied to the axle around the pin using an oxy-acetylene torch fitted with a number 18 or 25 nozzle or, failing that, a powerful blowlamp. While the axle is still hot, strike the pin again.

If you are still unsuccessful you will probably be wishing that you had given the job to someone else, but don't give up—if all else fails the pin can be drilled out. Use a drill well below the diameter of the pin to avoid damaging the bore in the axle beam and work from the unthreaded end.

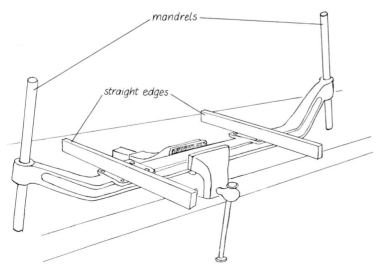

Fig. 4:3. **Two straight edges and two mandrels are needed to test a beam axle for straightness**

Fig. 4:4. An adjustable reamer is used on this Trojan stub axle

When you have a hole right through the pin, it can be enlarged gradually until only a thin shell remains. Then it should be possible to drive out the remains of the pin from the threaded end, collapsing it inwards as you go. You will also need a big hammer, a 4 lb (2 kg) club is ideal, and a large punch to drive the king pin out of the axle beam, again using the anvil for support—unless you enjoy the luxury of a press to push it out.

When you have removed the king pins, noting the position of any thrust washers or bearings (most likely to be above the bottom bush), and have separated the stub axles from the axle beam, clean everything with paraffin. Unscrew the grease nipples from the stub axles and, using a press or a vice, push out the bushes, noting the position of any flanges and oil or grease holes. Mechanics sometimes use sockets to drive out bushes, but I don't like this method. Apart from abusing the tools, hammering may cause dangerous chips to fly from the hardened sockets, putting your eyesight at risk. Instead use a piece of heavy steel bar or tubing. Reverse the process to fit the new bushes, aligning any grease or oil holes as you do so. If oil holes are needed but the bushes are not drilled, this should be done next, using a drill well below the root diameter to avoid damaging the grease-nipple threads in the stub axle.

The *vital* part of the job is to ream the bushes to size. The object is to make the pin a firm push fit in both bushes. There should be no play in either, nor must the pin tighten up appreciably as it enters the second bush. This would indicate that the two holes are out of alignment. If a plain reamer is to be used, make sure its flutes are clean and that it is well lubricated with a light oil. Then, applying a light, constant pressure, push it through the stub-axle bushes while turning it clockwise with a tap wrench. It is *not* a good idea to ream the bushes with the pin axis horizontal or to use an adjustable spanner to turn the reamer.

The plain reamer is a fairly straightforward tool. Provided you don't allow it to wobble and you turn it smoothly as it cuts, a good result will be obtained. The adjustable reamer allows some variation in size and is an excellent device, but its use requires a little more care. It has several hardened steel blades which slide in tapered slots in the shank; the tool's diameter increases as the blades are moved towards the squared driving end. Special cupped lock nuts are provided at each end to hold the blades firmly in place.

Before using an adjustable reamer, check that it is clean and well lubricated with a light oil, such as '3-In-One'. Adjust its diameter so that with the pilot inserted in the opposite bush, long end first, the reamer will enter the bush to be cut by approximately 1 in. (25 mm). Then, holding the pilot firmly in place, turn the reamer clockwise, applying a light-to-moderate force, until it passes through the bush. Withdraw the reamer, continuing to turn it clockwise and making sure that the pilot remains in place. This procedure is repeated for the other bush, and the bore diameter is gradually increased until the pin can be pushed through both bushes with a firm, steady hand.

Reassembly on to the axle beam is a reversal of the dismantling process with a few provisos:

1. All swarf should be removed and the bushes lubricated with the grease you intend to use in service.
2. Any thrust washers or bearings should be renewed and the vertical movement checked. This is not as critical as, say, engine or gearbox endfloats, but should not exceed 0.015–0.02 in. (0.4–0.5 mm). On a very old axle you may have to add an extra washer to achieve this.
3. After assembly make sure the stub axles move throughout their range of travel with no more than a light drag. Pump in some grease through the newly refitted nipples, and reinstall the assembly under the vehicle.

Some post-war cars with independent suspension employed a stepped king pin with its larger diameter and consequently larger bushes at the bottom where the wear is usually greater. Both bushes were reamed in one operation using a special double-diameter reamer sold as a special tool by the car manufacturer. The main applications of this idea were on the Austin 'County' series and BMC/BL cars. If you need one of these tools, an appropriate one-make club, such as the Austin Counties Car Club, may be able to help.

When king pins are used with independent front

Fig. 4:5. There should be no appreciable 'shake' of the female-threaded trunnion on a screwed steering swivel such as that found on a Morris Minor. If wear is evident, threads can be re-cut

suspension, the reaming process is much the same as for the beam axle arrangement, but the method of removing the stub axles will be different. The golden rule, as with suspension work, is to have a proper regard for the main springs. Ways of dealing with these potential killers are described in chapter 8, which should be read before attempting to release a coil spring.

Screwed steering swivels, such as those used by the Morris Minor and its cousins the Wolseley 1500 and the Riley 1.5, will have a long life if they are regularly and thoroughly greased. This means jacking the car up so that the weight is taken off the swivel threads and pumping grease in until it comes out *through* the swivel (*not* oozing from under or around the grease nipple, or pushing out a sealing plug). Originally, it was recommended that the Minor swivels were greased at 500-mile intervals. Later this was extended to 1000 and then to 3000 miles. However, I prefer a 1000-mile interval, especially if a long time is likely to elapse between greasings. The job may only take ten minutes or so, but if it is done regularly it will fend off, almost indefinitely, the need for expensive replacements.

The exact procedure for dismantling and reassembling screwed swivels will vary from one model of car to another, but with the Minor/Wolseley 1500/Riley 1.5 the car should be jacked up and supported on axle stands placed beneath the chassis legs so that the suspension torsion bars no longer support its weight. Next you will have to remove the road wheels, brake drums, hubs and brake back plates, releasing the hoses from the chassis brackets and removing the short bridge pipes between the wheel cylinders so that the back plates can be freed from the swivels. With all these out of the way the steering and suspension components will be much more visible.

Remove the rod between the front of the chassis and the lower suspension arm by undoing the bolt that passes through the rod and fork-ended bolt that connects the front and rear parts of the lower arm. By undoing three further nuts on the lower arm and taking the load of the torsion bar by placing a jack under the *rear* part of the lower arm and lifting it slightly, the front part of the lower arm can be removed. All that remains is to undo one nut from the front of the upper trunnion and disconnect the steering tie-rod ball joint to allow removal of the swivel assembly.

If you are satisfied that most or all of the wear is in the female-threaded trunnions, renew them using a service kit which will include trunnion pins and bushes, oil/grease seals, etc. However, if you are aiming for a high standard you cannot ignore the fact that the male threads on the swivel will probably be worn. This does not necessarily mean that it will have to be replaced. The threads can be re-cut to a smaller diameter using a special die which some Minor specialists may still hold, together with the necessary undersize trunnions. If you are fitting a new swivel you will have to transfer the stub axle from the old one to the new. It is best to use a press for this but not many amateurs enjoy such a luxury. If you have to use a hammer and drift, make sure they are substantial and that you support the swivel on an anvil or, at least, a substantial block of metal when you set about driving the stub out. Note that it is keyed in position. Reassembly is a reversal of the dismantling procedure, but don't forget to take the car to a garage afterwards for a check on the front wheel alignment.

Fig. 4:6. A $1\frac{1}{2}$ in. AF deep-socket will be needed to remove Mini and other BL steering-swivel ball joints

Renewing ball-type steering/suspension swivels

This later development not only simplified things mechanically, it also simplified steering-swivel renewal. The parts only needed to be replaced—no metal-cutting processes were required. If anyone should suggest that these joints can be adjusted for wear, I would remind them that such wear is a result of the ball becoming oval in shape; adjustment will lead to dangerous tight spots in the steering. Don't try it! It is often possible to renew ball-type swivels without disturbing the hubs or brake assemblies, but you do have to be careful not to let the weight of these swing on the brake hoses.

Ball-type swivels vary quite a lot. Two types used on cars popular with restorers are those of the Mini and other BMC/BL front-wheel-drive cars, and of the Jaguar Mk II range. The replacement of the ball joints on each of these will be looked at in more detail.

The Mini workshop manual says that two special tools are needed: one for compressing the rubber spring unit on cars with 'dry' suspension and a large socket (part number 18G 587) for unscrewing the ball-joint retainers. The former can be improvised from a length of $\frac{9}{16}$ in. steel rod, a nut and a tubular distance piece, and the latter, though not essential, will certainly make the job a lot easier. If the car has 'wet' suspension (Hydrolastic) a suspension pressurizing rig will also be required. The spring compressor fits beneath small plates, one on each side under the bonnet on top of the bulkhead. It is screwed into the spring and then the distance piece and nut are threaded on; the nut is screwed down, compressing the rubber spring just enough to clear the ball pins when they are released from their tapers.

By undoing the large screwed ball-joint retainers, the ball joints can be dismantled, revealing the ball pin which runs between the retainer and a smaller ball-pin seat. This is spring loaded in the lower joint. Overhaul kits containing all the parts needed are readily obtainable, so discard all of the old ones except, perhaps, the shims which might just be useful on reassembly. Fit the new parts to the swivel hubs (after cleaning the latter) except for the shims, lock rings for the retainers and the spring for the lower ball-pin retainer. Tighten each retainer in turn until the ball is just nipped, then measure the gap between the retainer and the swivel hub with a feeler gauge. The gap should be between 0.036 and 0.039 in. and is necessary to allow the fitting of the lock ring. If the gap is greater than specified, select shims to fit on top of the lock ring and bring the gap back within limits. Remove the retainer and fit the lock ring and shims, securing the former with the grease nipple. Pack the joint with grease and remember to refit the spring in the lower joint before replacing the retainer and tightening it to 70–80 lb ft with a torque wrench. A 'wet' suspension system will need re-pressurizing after renewal of the ball joints, and while the car is at the garage it is a good idea to have the wheel alignment checked in case the work has upset it.

The Jaguar front suspension has a non-adjustable upper-wishbone ball joint which is fairly easy to change without the need for special tools, although the ability to wield a big hammer is an asset. The road wheel is removed after jacking up under the *lower* wishbone. Then the nut securing the upper wishbone to the stub-axle carrier is unscrewed until it is flush with the end of the ball-pin thread. The pin must then be driven off its taper—I recommend a 2 lb (1 kg) ball pein hammer for this, used with a hefty drift of about 1 in. (25 mm) diameter so that you can bring some 'beef' to bear. Once the pin is released, remove its nut and the two bolts clamping it between the wishbone arms, but make a careful note of the positions of

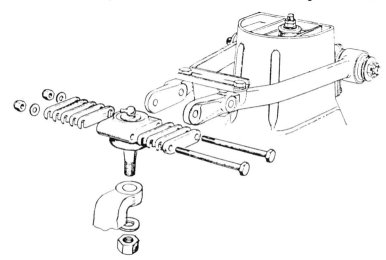

Fig. 4:7. This upper ball joint on a Mk II Jaguar is not adjustable and must therefore be replaced if worn. When doing so be careful to keep all castor shims in their original position (courtesy of Jaguar Cars Ltd)

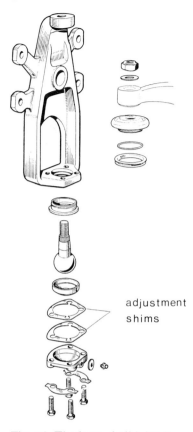

adjustment
shims

Fig. 4:8. The lower ball joint is, however, adjustable with the use of shims (courtesy of Jaguar Cars Ltd)

the shims and packing pieces. If the latter are reassembled incorrectly, the castor setting will be wrong. Assembly is a reversal of the dismantling procedure.

The job of renewing the lower-wishbone ball joint is a bit more complicated and, once again, it is helpful if you can swing a big hammer in a confined space. If you are renewing the top and bottom ball joints at the same time, which is most likely, don't tighten the top ball pin fully on to its taper; just insert the pin in the stub axle and screw the nut on a few threads. Remove the brake caliper and hang it from some part of the car so that the flexible brake hose is not strained; remove the wheel hub, brake disc and dirt shield. Then free the bottom ball pin from its taper in the same manner as for the top joint. After removing the nut you can take the stub-axle carrier to the bench where you can work in comfort.

Dismantling the joint proper entails removing four bolts, a metal cap and a rubber gaiter. This reveals the hard plastic bottom cup (a socket in Jaguar parlance), its upper cup (which they call a spigot), the ball pin and a series of shims. The new parts are fitted with a full quota of shims which are taken out one at a time until the pin begins to nip. Then shims of 0.004–0.006 in. (0.1–0.15 mm) are fitted so that it can be moved by hand.

All of these jobs, which are done with the aid of a jack which simultaneously lifts the car and compresses the powerful road spring, should be made safe by placing an axle stand or some substantial baulks of wood beneath a safe part of the car and virtually touching it to catch it should it slip off the jack. Bear in mind the points made earlier about steering geometry, and if the top wishbone is taken off completely make sure the distance pieces and shims that control the camber angle at the inner end are put back where they came from.

There are numerous arrangements of ball swivel and hybrid pin-and-ball designs, and I hope this description of tackling two forms may give some general guidance which will be useful. Finally, there are various strut suspensions attributed to MacPherson or Chapman, but since these also constitute the front suspension dampers, I will deal with them when discussing suspension overhaul.

Chapter 5 | Adjusting and overhauling steering mechanisms

With a few exceptions, the steering mechanisms you encounter will be either of the rack-and-pinion type or steering boxes.

Rack-and-pinion steering has a pinion (or gear wheel) attached to the steering wheel via a steering shaft and meshed with a toothed bar called a rack. Rotary motion of the pinion is converted into sideways movement of the rack. This, acting through the track rods, moves the steering arms which turn the stub axles carrying the road wheels. In contrast, all of the steering boxes rely on the screw-thread principle for their operation, but the enthusiast encountering these for the first time, in workshop manuals or whatever, may be bewildered by the variety of names which are used.

Probably one of the most common steering boxes is the cam-and-peg type. The 'cam' is in fact a large screw thread attached to the end of the steering shaft and the peg, which meshes with the cam, is attached to an arm forming the upper part of a rocker shaft. As the cam is turned by the steering wheel, the peg moves one way or the other along the cam, causing the rocker shaft to turn through an arc. This motion is relayed to a drop-arm which moves a rod called a 'drag link'. This, in turn, moves the steering arms and stub axles. Alternatively, the motion may be relayed across the car to a steering idler arm mounted opposite the steering box, in which case the steering box directly operates the steering arm on the driver's side, and the idler and its linkage the steering arm on the passenger's side.

The different varieties of steering box will be examined in more detail later, but first let us consider adjustments. Wear in the steering mechanism, as in so many mechanical

Above **Fig. 5:1. The simple essentials of rack-and-pinion steering, the rack being the toothed bar**

Right **Fig. 5:2. Cam-and-peg steering, in this case a high-efficiency unit. Note the spring-loaded adjusting screw at the top (see text)**

components, does not take place evenly. Almost all of the steering wheel movement done by the driver takes place a few degrees either side of the straight-ahead position, so this is where the wear is concentrated. This is taken into consideration by the makers of steering gears who set the initial meshing of the parts so that they are 'tighter' in the straight-ahead position than on full lock.

When adjusting a steering box or rack-and-pinion mechanism, the object is to minimize free-play without creating any tight spots. This is very important. The slightest of tight spots will make the car difficult to steer and potentially dangerous. It should also be understood that the amount of free-play at the steering wheel will be much greater with a steering box than with rack-and-pinion steering. Up to 3 in. (75 mm) at the steering wheel rim is acceptable where a steering box is used but only $\frac{1}{2}$ in. (13 mm) for a rack-and-pinion mechanism.

Fig. 5:3. It is a good idea to mark the position of a steering wheel before removing it from its shaft

Adjustment should be carried out with the front of the car lifted off the ground and supported on axle stands. As adjustment proceeds, the steering wheel should be turned with the fingertips through about 30 degrees to each side of the straight-ahead position, feeling for the point at which the slightest tendency to 'run tight' first occurs. Then the adjustment should be backed off very slightly so that the tightness *just* disappears. This work in the garage should be followed by a road test to make sure that there are definitely no tight spots. Adjustment is bound to be a compromise; it is better to accept some free movement than to use the car with tight spots in the steering.

On many steering boxes, adjustment is effected by a simple screw which pushes the steering rocker shaft downwards, tightening the mesh, but in some instances it is necessary to remove shims from beneath the top cover to remove free-play. Some steering boxes have a small screw and spring at the end of the adjusting screw which must be removed before carrying out the adjustment. Sometimes rack-and-pinion mechanisms can be tightened by increasing the pressure on the damper pad to make the pinion mesh more closely with the rack. Usually this is done by removing a shim; however, care must be taken to ensure that steering wheel movement is not stiffened unduly.

Fig. 5:4. Before removing the drop-arm from its shaft, identify its markings. On the arm of this Mk II Jaguar there are marks for both left- and right-hand drive. This is positioned for right-hand drive and would need to be re-positioned for left-hand drive

Whilst some means of adjustment is normally provided for the steering shaft as well as the rocker (or sector) shaft, it is not usually accessible without removing the steering mechanism from the car or, in some cases, removing the steering wheel.

Removing the unit from the car

The exact technique followed will vary according to the make of car and its age. Many early post-war cars employed wooden toe- and floorboards, which meant that the steering box, column, steering wheel and drop-arm could be pulled back into the car after removing the toe-boards and sometimes the pedals (or at least their pads). Cars of this period often had horn and indicator wires led through the hollow steering shaft in a thin metal 'mast', so it is necessary to label each of them for reassembly.

On cars with unitary construction the steering wheel must be removed if the steering box and column are assembled as a unit, which is the case for most cars of the 1950s and early 1960s. Before removing the wheel, its position relative to the shaft should be recorded for reassembly, either by placing the road wheels so that they point straight ahead and noting the position of the steering wheel spokes, or by 'dot punching' the steering wheel hub and its shaft.

In some cases where the horn and indicator controls are at the centre of the stationary wheel hub, the mast carrying the wires must be removed before the wheel can be taken off. This needs to be done with some care to avoid a lot of tedious fiddling later on. Usually there are three indicator wires (green, green/red and green/white), plus one or two horn wires running through the mast and passing through the bottom cover of the steering box. To remove the mast the wires must be disconnected and a clamp released. The latter can be of the split variety or, sometimes, take the form of an 'olive' which is compressed on to the mast by a nut in a similar way to a domestic plumbing joint. Before removing the mast, it is a good idea to bind the disconnected wiring snap connectors with a thin wire which is led through the steering column as the mast is taken out. Subsequently it can be used to assist in threading them back through. As the mast is removed oil will run out of the steering box, so you must have a suitable container ready to catch it. Clean the wires carefully so that the colour coding is clearly visible for reassembly.

If it is necessary to take off the drop-arm before removing the steering box, disconnect the steering link and mark the arm's position relative to its shaft before doing so. I would not recommend that you try removing the arm without a suitable extractor—you might cause damage that you would regret afterwards. *Avoid the temptation to use a hammer.* If, with the extractor tightened fully, the arm still does not budge, try heating the arm where the rocker shaft passes through it. This will expand the arm and release its taper from the shaft. Then the steering box can be unbolted and removed. In some cases, the distributor, starter motor or radiator may have to be removed to give clearance.

Later cars with steering boxes tend to have a joint in the steering shaft which can be undone to make removal easier. Another improvement was the removal of electrical switches from the wheel centre, making work in this area a lot easier.

Where steering is by rack-and-pinion, you can often take the unit away and leave the steering column in place.

Fig. 5:5. Set the steering wheel in the straight-ahead position and have the rack centralized before removing and refitting

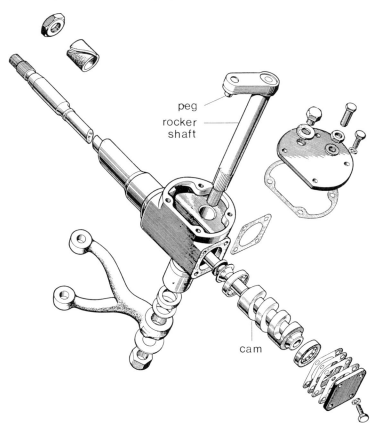

peg
rocker
shaft

cam

Fig. 5:6. A simple cam-and-peg system as found on the Austin A30 (courtesy of Austin Rover Ltd)

Before doing so, mark the coupling device in some way to ensure correct reassembly.

Once the steering box or rack-and-pinion unit is out of the car, clean off all the road dirt with paraffin. Take off the top cover in the case of a steering box, or the damper plate or plug on a rack-and-pinion unit, and drain out as much oil as possible.

Overhauling steering boxes

With the drop-arm and steering wheel out of the way, dismantling can begin. The procedure will vary a little according to type, there having been four types in common use since the 1930s. You might meet any of the following:

1. Cam-and-peg steering

Often of Cam Gears Ltd manufacture, this typically had a

spiral cam or 'worm' supported on ball races at either end of the steering box and, at right angles to it, a rocker shaft carrying an arm and a peg which engaged with the cam. The rocker shaft was carried in bushes and had an oil seal at its outer end. Attached to the shaft by a taper and a key, or by a tapered spline, was the drop-arm (still occasionally referred to as a Pitman arm). The steering shaft was supported at the top of the column by a felt bush.

Dismantling is quite easy. Once the top cover is off (take care not to lose any shims, and keep the gasket—you might have to make a replacement), the rocker shaft can be pushed or lightly driven out. Usually four screws retain the end cover which should be removed carefully. Collect the

Above left **Fig. 5:7. The first step of assembly is to refit the upper steering-box ball bearings. They can be held in place in the cup with either Vaseline or grease. That is also the method used for holding them to the screwdriver during assembly**

Above **Fig. 5:8. Enter the steering shaft vertically into its upper bearing**

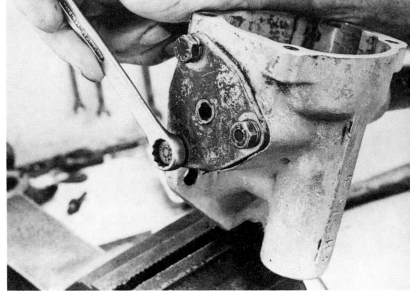

Above **Fig. 5:9.** With the box held in a vice the shaft can be pulled home prior to the fitment of the lower bearing

Above right **Fig. 5:10.** The lower bearing is followed by the cover complete with the adjustment shims

shims beneath the cover and the balls from the lower bearing as you do so. Then remove the inner bearing cups, worm and steering shaft as an assembly, catching the balls from the upper bearing as it comes out. Now you can inspect the parts and decide what needs to be done.

After prolonged use, the bush or bushes carrying the rocker shaft will almost certainly have worn. You may be able to get someone with a lathe to turn up some replacements, but if the bearing surfaces of the rocker shaft are worn the only alternative to replacement is to build up the shaft by some metal-depositing method, such as spraying or plating, and regrind it.

In cam-and-peg boxes the steering-shaft bearings are usually a pair of angular-contact ball races with uncaged balls. The balls will be a standard size and easy to obtain, possibly from a cycle dealer but certainly from a bearing specialist. However, the cups and cones forming the outer and inner parts will be much more difficult to find. In some instances the bearing cones are integral with the cam on the steering shaft and are not replaceable. These parts, like the steering cam and the peg which engages with it, are hardened and have a good wear resistance, but *any* pitting or breaking up of the hard skin will cause harsh and potentially dangerous operation. Any parts with this sort of damage must be replaced.

When reassembling the box, carefully drive or press the outer cup for the upper bearing into its housing, ensuring that it is kept square and is fully home. Pack its bearing surface with petroleum jelly to hold the balls in place. Then insert the balls and hold the assembly with the steering column vertical while the shaft is carefully placed into it. Fit the balls to the lower cup with petroleum jelly and, with the box horizontal on the bench and the steering shaft held firmly home to prevent loss of balls from the upper bearing, lightly tap or push the lower cup home. When the end cover is fitted, shims must be added or removed so that the shaft turns freely with no end-play and no 'preload'; i.e. the lengthways movement of the steering shaft must just be taken out and no more.

Assuming that the rocker-shaft bush is in good condition or that it has been renewed and reamed to size, refitting the shaft is straightforward. It is followed by the top cover. The adjusting screw should be set so that there is *just* perceptible end-play on the shaft in the straight-ahead position, final adjustment being carried out when the unit is back in the car.

A variant of the cam-and-peg arrangement is the 'high-efficiency cam-and-peg steering' (Figs. 5:2, 5:11), the peg of which is carried in a ball or roller race so that it is free to turn. This reduces friction, making the steering lighter and reducing wear. Normally both peg and bearing are held in place by a circlip, making replacement a simple matter. This type often has a spring-loaded, rocker-shaft adjuster. It should be adjusted with the spring removed.

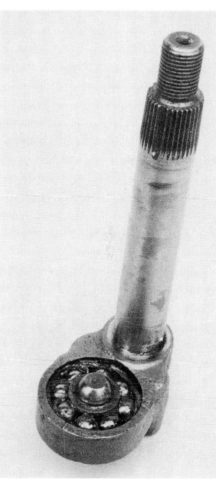

Fig. 5:11. The peg on this high-efficiency unit rotates on balls in the arm on the rocker shaft

2. Worm-and-nut steering

In this type a nut, usually made of bronze, moves up and down a worm (on the end of the steering shaft) as the steering wheel is turned. A peg on the rocker shaft is linked to the nut and follows its movement, causing the shaft to move through an arc. In some instances the nut is prevented from rotating by a dowel which fits into a groove machined along its length (as shown in Fig. 5:13), in which

Fig. 5:12. A rocker shaft being fitted into the box. Note the peg is retained by a circlip

case the peg moves in a transverse slot. Another version has its peg inserted into a spherical steel cup pushed into the nut, so that the nut oscillates as the rocker shaft moves in an arc.

Dismantling the worm-and-nut box is only a little different from the cam-and-peg type. The top cover is taken off and the rocker shaft removed. The end cover follows and, by turning the steering shaft, the steering nut is unscrewed from the worm. By unscrewing the lock nut at the top of the column and the adjusting nut (carefully catching the ball bearings), the steering shaft can be removed.

The steering nut may have become worn on its outer surface or on its thread and, like the previous box, wear may have occurred on the rocker shaft and in its bush. To assess the wear, clean the parts, reassemble them temporarily and attempt to move the rocker arm and the nut radially. Only slight movement is acceptable.

Rebuild the box in a reversal of the dismantling procedure, adjusting the bearing at the top of the column to just eliminate lengthways movement after the box is assembled. As with the previous type, final adjustment of the rocker shaft is best carried out at the straight-ahead position with the box installed in the car.

3. Recirculating-ball steering

This is a de luxe version of the worm-and-nut type. Friction is reduced considerably by a continuously recirculating chain of steel balls which run in specially shaped threads between the worm and its nut. When the balls reach the end of the nut they travel through a transfer tube back to the other end. The transfer tube is often fabricated from light sheet metal but sometimes it may be formed within the nut.

The recirculating-ball unit is dealt with in a similar manner to the previous types. If, as is often the case, the box is coupled to the steering shaft at or near its entry point, the worm shaft will be supported on opposed bearings similar to the cam-and-peg arrangement. Begin by taking off the top cover, collecting the gasket and making sure that the spring and button from the rocker-

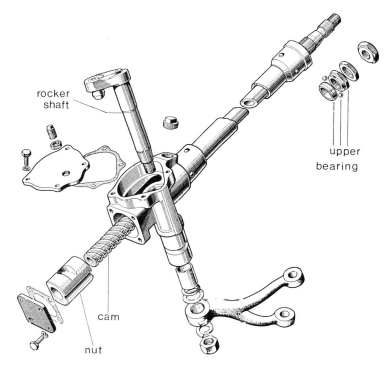

rocker
shaft

upper
bearing

cam

nut

shaft adjuster are not lost. With the top cover off, the steering-column (or upper) end cover is removed together with its gaskets and any shims or spacer. Push the worm shaft up enough to free the upper race and its balls, collecting them carefully. Then unscrew the worm from the nut and lift both clear. Remove the remaining (lower) end cover, its bearing cup and balls. By taking off the transfer tube, the balls inside the nut can be removed for inspection.

By now you will be familiar with the general procedure for inspection. Once again you will be looking for wear on the steering-shaft ball bearings, the rocker shaft and its bush and, additionally, on the balls which run between the nut and the worm. Reject any balls or tracks which are pitted or rough. This applies also to the roller (see Fig. 5:15) between the nut and the rocker shaft.

Begin reassembly by fitting the transfer tube to the nut and filling the tube with the balls; the remaining balls are grease-packed into the grooves in the upper part of the nut.

Fig. 5:13. The worm-and-nut steering box was an alternative fitment on the A30. The nut, as well as turning the rocker shaft as it moves on its thread, acts as a lower bearing for the steering shaft. An upper bearing, just under the steering wheel, controls the endfloat of the shaft (courtesy of Austin Rover Ltd)

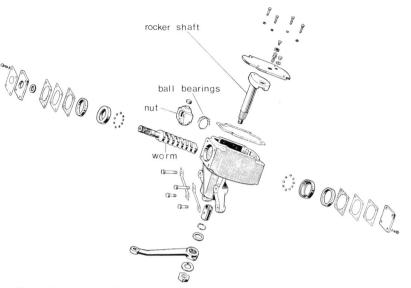

rocker shaft

ball bearings

nut

worm

Fig. 5:14. The recirculating-ball steering box, as found on the Mk II Jaguar, is a sophisticated version of the worm-and-nut system. The nut is carried on ball bearings to minimize friction (courtesy of Jaguar Cars Ltd)

Carefully start the worm shaft in the nut and then screw on the latter for half the worm's length. Following this, the lower ball race should be grease-packed, its balls replaced and the assembly refitted. Use the shims and distance piece, originally fitted with a new gasket on each side of the shim pack. The worm and nut should be inserted through the upper bearing aperture and into the lower bearing, being very careful not to dislodge any of the loose balls. Tape over the serrated spline on the worm shaft to protect its seal during reassembly. Pack the upper race with grease, add the bearings and fit it together with the shims and distance pieces in their original positions. A new gasket should be included on each side of the shims.

When the bolts at each end of the box are tightened, the bearings of the worm shaft should have a 0.002–0.003 in. (0.05–0.075 mm) preload obtained by adding or subtracting 0.005 in. (0.13 mm) shims or 0.003 in. (0.075 mm) gaskets, remembering that there must always be a gasket at each side of the shim pack. With the bolts at one end fully tightened and those at the other end lightly tightened until there is no end-play, it should be possible to insert a 0.002 or 0.003 in. (0.05 or 0.075 mm) feeler gauge between the end plate and the casing. Then tighten the bolts fully. Check that the worm shaft turns smoothly and easily

before fitting the rocker shaft. Engage the slot in the rocker shaft with the peg on the worm nut, fit the roller over the peg, fit the cover and insert the four bolts and tighten them. Finally, before refitting the spring and button to the rocker-shaft adjuster, set the steering in the straight-ahead position and lightly tighten the rocker-shaft adjusting screw until there is no play on the shaft. Tighten the lock nut and replace the spring and button. The unit is now ready for refitting to the car, where any final adjustment of the rocker shaft can be carried out.

4. Hour-glass worm-and-roller steering

This is a high-quality system giving low levels of friction and high efficiency. One of the virtues of this design is that it can be of the variable (or more accurately, varying) ratio type. The procedures for dismantling and overhaul follow the pattern described for the other steering boxes, but there are three areas of adjustment—for worm-shaft endfloat, for rocker-shaft endfloat, and for depth of mesh between the roller and the worm.

Worm-shaft endfloat is adjusted (as with previous types) by removing or exchanging shims until there is zero endfloat and zero preload. Rocker-shaft endfloat adjustment is a simple screw and lock-nut affair. It should be

Above left **Fig. 5:15.** In this view of the Jaguar system, the arm of the rocker shaft (a), its roller (b), nut (c) and worm (d) can be seen, as can the adjusting screw (e) and its lock nut. The screwed plug (f) over the spring must be removed during adjustment

Above **Fig. 5:16.** This hour-glass worm-and-roller steering box is from an Aston Martin. The worm is on the right, note the wear on its ball race, and the roller and upper part of the rocker shaft are on the left. Removing shims puts the roller into deeper mesh with the worm

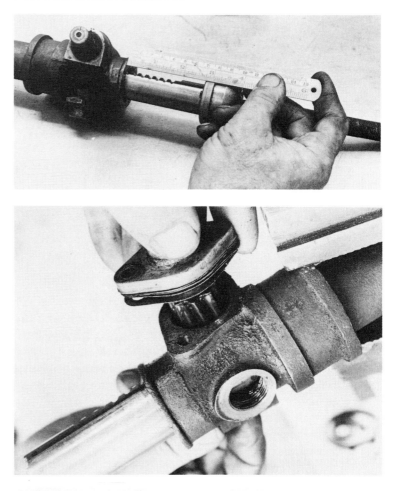

Fig. 5:17. This Morris Minor rack is centralized in its housing by measuring at either end

Fig. 5:18. Removing the pinion shaft, its end bearing and shims

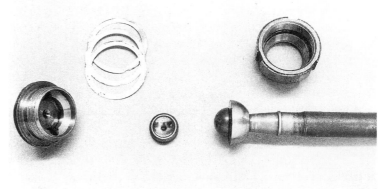

Fig. 5:19. The components of a ball joint on which the side rods turn. They are adjusted with shims and a light force should be needed to move the rods

adjusted to give no end-play and no preload, but if there is still movement at the steering wheel, the rocker-shaft roller must be moved into a tighter mesh with the cam in the straight-ahead position. This is achieved by removing or exchanging shims behind the rocker-shaft thrust washers.

Overhauling rack-and-pinion mechanisms

Rack-and-pinion units of the non-powered variety are fairly straightforward to dismantle and reassemble. However, whether the home restorer will be able to buy parts over the counter is very much another matter.

There are two main types of rack-and-pinion steering gear: those in which the rack forms the centre of a three-piece steering system with two short track rods attached to its ends (well-known 'classic' cars using this system are the MGA, Morris Minor and Triumph Spitfire, Stag, etc.), and the two-piece steering system with two long track rods attached to the centre of the rack, which can be found on the Hillman Imp and its derivatives and the Riley RM series. Apart, perhaps, from the manufacture of a couple of special 'C' spanners for undoing and adjusting the inner ball joints of some units, none of these should present any difficulty to the amateur mechanic with some experience. However, the manufacturers of the Hillman Imp advise against dismantling and overhaul if a replacement unit is available.

Early examples of the first type of rack-and-pinion unit described, like that fitted to the Morris Minor, had plain bearings on the pinion shaft and an unbushed rack. They are easy to dismantle and reassemble. After removing the ball-pin track-rod ends, release the rubber gaiters by undoing their clips. Watch for oil running out of the rack at this stage. Next wipe clean the exposed ends of the rack and centralize it by making sure that the distances between the backs of the inner ball joints and the rack housing are equal at both ends. Examine the end of the pinion shaft and its housing which may be marked to correspond to this position. If they are not, some form of indelible marking is needed so that they can be reassembled in the right position. Provided both surfaces are grease-free, typists' correcting fluid works well.

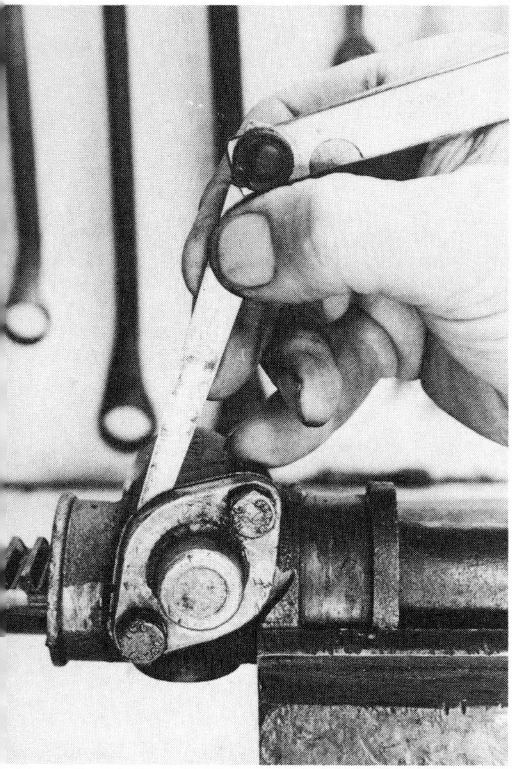

Fig. 5:20. Pinion endfloat can be checked with a feeler gauge

You will need a 'C' spanner to unscrew the inner ball joints which come off as an assembly with their track rods. Next take out the pinion end damper pad by undoing a large domed nut and collecting the pad, its spring and shims, followed by the auxiliary damper at the other end.

After removing the pinion-shaft tail bearing and, again, carefully collecting the shims, you can remove the pinion shaft and prise out its oil seal. All that remains is to pull out the rack by its toothed end. Although it isn't strictly essential to do this on early units, later examples with soft bushes at the opposite end to the pinion housing may be damaged by the rack teeth if it is pulled out in the other direction.

Later units featuring ball-bearing pinion shafts may provide a slight additional difficulty since the balls and cups must be collected carefully during dismantling. In most cases the upper (steering-shaft side) bearing cup, or outer race, cannot be removed until the rack has been taken out.

After cleaning everything in paraffin, begin your inspection. Look for wear on the bush, if one is fitted, on the back of the rack and in the housings. Check for chipping or surface break-up on ball bearings and for chipped or worn teeth on the rack and pinion themselves. Wear may appear as a 'wavy' surface on the teeth. Ball bearings will be easily obtainable, but the other parts will be more difficult to find—unless your car is a late 'classic' or perhaps a Minor or MG.

Reassembly of the earlier version is exemplified by the following procedure for the Morris Minor. First the ball joint and track rod at one end of the rack are assembled to it with a new lock washer. The joint is adjusted by the progressive removal of shims until it is no longer 'floppy'; it should be just too stiff to fall under its own weight. If it is very stiff in places and loose in others, a new ball housing and seat or a complete new assembly will be needed. Tighten the joint to the rack and lock it by punching the washer into the grooves provided in the ball housing. Grease and insert the rack, then refit the other track rod and ball joint.

Centralize the rack by adjusting the distances between

Fig. 5:21. Pinion-shaft damper
with adjustment shims

the back of each ball-joint lock washer and the adjacent end of the rack housing until they are equal. After fitting the upper (thick) thrust washer, insert the pinion so that when it is home the marks made previously on both pinion and housing are in alignment. Next set the pinion endfloat to 0.002 in. (0.05 mm) by removing shims and checking with a dial gauge. The other way is to assemble the pinion tail bearing without shims and lightly nip its bolts, measuring the clearance between the body of the bearing with a feeler gauge. After dismantling the assembly, shims equal to the measured clearance plus 0.002 in. (0.05 mm) are fitted and the bolts tightened. Don't forget to insert the lower pinion thrust washer, bevelled side to the pinion, for this setting. If you have neither a dial gauge nor a micrometer to measure the shims, but have reasonably sensitive fingers and hearing, make adjustments until free-play is *just* perceptible by feel and by 'ear'.

After fitting the gaiters (new ones if you can get them), adjust the pinion damper by assembling the domed cover and plunger without shims or spring and tightening it progressively until it is just possible to turn the pinion by pulling the rack through its housing. Measure the clearance between the domed cover and the rack housing with feelers. Then remove the cover and refit it with shims equal to the measured clearance plus 0.002 in. (0.05 mm), and its plunger and spring. After fitting the track-rod ends and replacing the pinion oil seal, the unit is ready for refitting.

The ball-bearing pinion shafts of later units are usually lightly preloaded on assembly. This is done *after* fitting the rack, with a new bush if necessary, and the pinion. The pinion end cover, which retains the lower (or tail) bearing, is fitted initially without any shims or gasket and the bolts are lightly tightened. The gap between the cover and the housing is measured with a feeler gauge. Then the cover is removed, shims and a gasket equal to the gap minus about 0.002 in. (0.05 mm) are fitted and the cover bolted up tight.

Generally, SAE 90 or 140 oil is used to lubricate the rack-and-pinion units. Early examples are charged through a nipple (on the nearside on a Minor), using a grease gun filled with oil. Later units are pre-lubricated before fitting the gaiters by holding the rack housing upright and pouring in about ½ pint (300 cc) of oil. It is worth fitting new gaiters as they are prone to perishing and splitting.

The other type of rack-and-pinion gear, having its track rods attached at the centre, is much less common than the first, but it is overhauled along similar lines. The Riley unit, for example, is dismantled as follows:

1. Remove the track-rod inner ball pins by jarring them off their tapers.
2. Remove the mounting bracket at the opposite end to the pinion housing.
3. Remove the countersunk screws from the collar, detach the rubber cover and knock the collar away.
4. Lightly drive out the end bearing housing together with its spherical bush.
5. Turn the bush through 90 degrees and pull it out through the slots in the housing.
6. Remove the damper plunger housing with its plunger, shims and spring after releasing the three nuts.
7. Remove the three screws from the pinion cover and take off the cover and shims. Pull out the pinion and its taper-roller bearings.

8. Detach the rubber gaiter from the rack housing and pull out the rack with its double track-rod eye. The latter can be unscrewed from the rack if necessary.

Reassembly is a reversal of the dismantling procedure, carrying out shim adjustments to the pinion shaft and its damper along similar lines to the previous type.

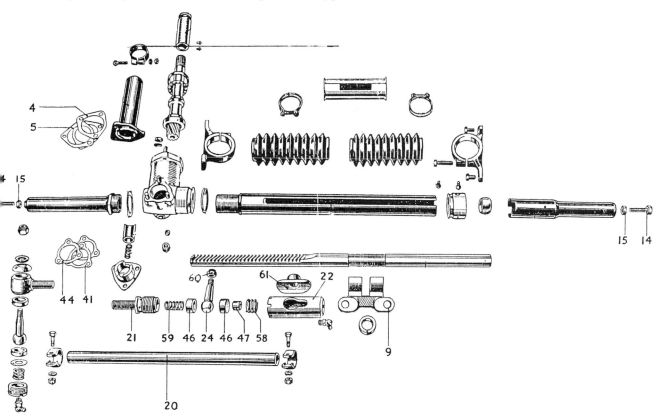

Fig. 5:22. The Riley RM rack-and-pinion mechanism differs from the Morris Minor in that the side rods (20) connect to the centre of the rack at the double eye (9) via the sundry parts (21, 59, 46, 24, 47, 58, 22, 60 and 61) and in numerous details. Pinion-shaft endfloat is controlled by shims (4 and 5), damping by shims (41 and 44) and steering lock by screws and lock nuts (14 and 15) (courtesy of Austin Rover Ltd)

Chapter 6 | Power-assisted steering

Introduced in the late 1950s on British cars, early users being Jaguar, Armstrong Siddeley, Humber and Vauxhall, power-assisted steering gained in popularity and by the late 1960s/early 1970s many cars were equipped with it. However, a lot of enthusiasts regard the power-assistance system with apprehension, as something of a mystery, like automatic transmission or fuel injection. I hope this chapter will remove some of that apprehension by providing an understanding of how the system works, the maintenance required, fault diagnosis and the repairs and overhaul procedures within the scope of the amateur mechanic.

The essentials of power-assisted steering are as follows:

1. A source of power. This is an engine-driven hydraulic pump generating up to 1500 psi (105 bar) maximum pressure.
2. A control valve responsive to the steering wheel movement and torque.
3. A servo cylinder to apply the power, either integral with a steering box or, less commonly, an external ram fixed between the vehicle's frame and the steering linkage.

Pumps

Several types of pump have been used for power steering. The Hoburn Eaton double-rotor pump may be familiar to home mechanics since it is also widely used as an engine oil pump. Some systems have vane pumps which are used for engine lubrication too. Probably the most widely used pump, however, is the roller type. All the pumps rely on some sort of eccentric rotor moving within the pump body to create alternately increasing and decreasing volumes that give the pumping action.

The Hoburn Eaton pump has two lobed rotors turning one within the other, the inner rotor being driven by the engine and, in turn, driving the outer. The former has one less lobe than the latter so that as it makes one revolution it 'overtakes' one lobe on the outer. This action causes the volume between the rotors to increase when they are opposite the inlet port and decrease when they are opposite the delivery port. Thus fluid enters, is pressurized and delivered.

The vane pump has a number of vanes engaged in a rotor and revolving in a casing which is eccentric to the rotor. As the distance between the edge of the rotor and the case increases, the inlet port is uncovered and fluid allowed to enter. As it decreases the delivery port is uncovered and the fluid ejected. In power steering the vane pump is generally 'pressure balanced', having an elliptical casing with two inlet and two delivery ports so that pressure is developed simultaneously on both sides. This prevents a heavy side load on the bearings.

The roller pump has a rotor carrying a number of rollers. As the rotor turns, each roller is forced outwards against the eccentric casing, creating a space and hence a depression behind, which draws fluid into the casing. As the volume decreases with continuing rotation, the fluid is pressurized and forced through the delivery port.

Valves

Several types of valve are used, controlled by compression springs or torsion bars. Owing to space limitations, I will consider two typical versions. The simpler of the two is the spool valve.

In the form shown (Fig. 6:5), the valve, which has two grooves machined in its surface and three interconnecting internal drillings, moves in a housing having four ports (1, 2, 3, 4) and three annular grooves (X, Y, Z). The unit is for a left-hand-drive, rack-and-pinion system with the steering unit ahead of the front wheels and the valve assembly mounted below it. The valve, shown in its 'no assistance' position, is connected by a link to the pinion housing. The latter is not rigidly attached to the rack

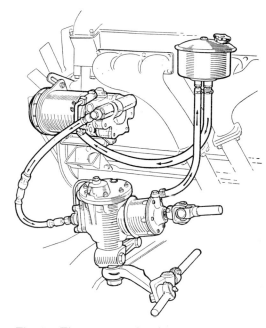

Fig. 6:1. The power-assisted steering system of a Mk II Jaguar. On early cars the pump was driven off the back of the dynamo but on later cars there was a separate drive (see Fig. 3:6) (courtesy of Jaguar Cars Ltd)

housing but can move slightly in either direction against springs. Fluid is pumped to port 2 in the valve housing and returns to the pump via a reservoir from port 3. Port 1 feeds servo chamber L in the steering unit and port 4 feeds chamber R. Admitting fluid to chamber L and exhausting chamber R moves the steering rack to the right and vice versa.

Rotation of the pinion shaft initially causes the pinion to 'walk' a short distance along the rack against the force of the centralizing springs (not shown). The pinion housing pivots about P, moving the link in the same direction as the rack. To move the rack to the right the valve is pulled slightly out of its bore. Fluid supply to port 4 and servo chamber R is reduced or even shut off, while that to port 1 and chamber L is increased through Y. At the same time the return route from port 4 to port 3 via the internal drilling and Z and X is opened up. The pressure imbalance at the servo piston causes the rack to move to the right. As the movement is completed, the rack housing and the control valve return to their central 'no assistance' position.

For a movement to the left, the valve is pushed into its bore so that the fluid supply to port 4 increases and that to port 1 is reduced, while the area of the return route from

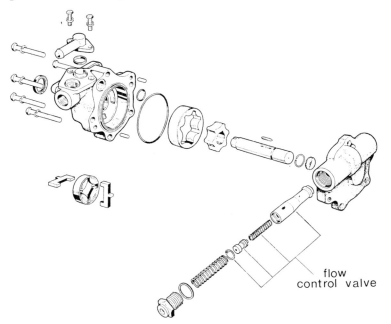

Fig. 6:2. The familiar Hoburn Eaton double-rotor pump is used for power steering amongst other things and in this application a flow control valve is needed (courtesy of Jaguar Cars Ltd)

flow
control valve

port 1 to port 3 is increased. Pressure rises in R, falls in L and the rack moves to the left.

Since the movement of the pinion housing is a reaction to the resistance to rack movement, its travel against the springs (and hence valve travel and the assistance given) will depend on the grip between the tyres and the road.

The second popular valve is the rotary version tensioned by a torsion bar. The Marles design is illustrated in Figs. 6:6 and 6:7. The cylindrical valve comprises an outer sleeve attached to the worm and an inner rotor connected to the steering shaft. These are joined by a torsion bar of 0.242 in. (6 mm) diameter. Oil is supplied from the pump to the large ports A and from there to three short grooves in the rotor. In the 'no assistance' position, low pressure occurs on both sides of the servo piston. Fluid is returned through the longer grooves B, collected at the upper end of the valve/rotor/worm assembly and returned to the pump to be filtered and recirculated.

With torque applied, the torsion bar is deflected so that the rotor moves relative to the sleeve; this has the effect of increasingly opening ports C to pump pressure and shutting them off from the return channels, while ports D are increasingly opened to the return lines and closed to pressure. The resulting pressure difference across the servo piston gives steering assistance proportional to the deflection of the torsion bar and hence steering torque. On the opposite turn the effects of rotor movement on ports C and D are reversed. In the unlikely event of a torsion bar breaking, safety splines connect the worm to the steering shaft with some 7 degrees of play between taking up movement in either direction.

Servo piston/cylinder arrangements

Perhaps the simplest power-assisted steering system, the in-line reactive ram has a valve and servo cylinder forming a single unit remote from the steering box. Fig. 6:8 shows how this unit was incorporated into Vauxhall cars. The servo cylinder and its valve can be overhauled or replaced without disturbing the steering box, which is a considerable advantage. However, the system does have the disadvantage of being responsive to drop-arm movement,

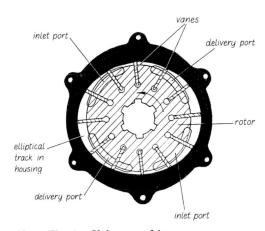

Above **Fig. 6:3. Volvo use this type of vane pump for power-assisted steering (pas)**

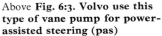

Below **Fig. 6:4. The Roller pump, however, is probably the most widely used (courtesy of Land Rover Ltd)**

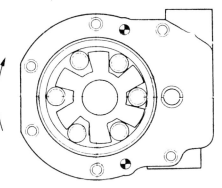

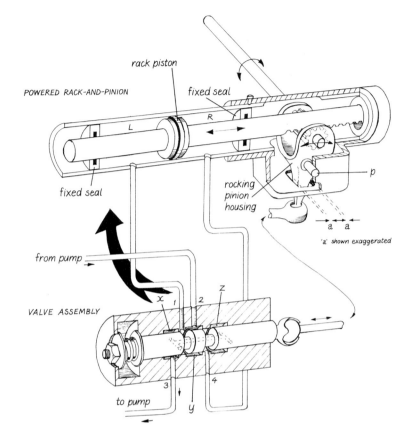

rack piston

POWERED RACK-AND-PINION   fixed seal

L   R

fixed seal

rocking
pinion
housing

p

a   a

'a' shown exaggerated

from pump

VALVE ASSEMBLY

x   1   2   z

3   4

to pump   y

Fig. 6:5. A spool valve is used with rack-and-pinion pas and in a slightly different form with in-line reactive units (see text)

that is, to the *output* from the steering box, whereas others are responsive to *input* from the steering wheel. This can cause a slight but disconcerting lag in power response.

In Marles steering gears of the hour-glass worm-and-roller type, the power cylinder is incorporated in the steering-box casing. It operates a toothed rack which engages with teeth on the rocker shaft to transmit force.

In Burman, Volvo and Mercedes units of the worm-and-nut type, the nut forms the servo piston and moves in a bore in the steering-box casing, applying power assistance directly within the box.

Fluid

The hydraulic fluid used in power-steering systems is automatic transmission fluid, a red mineral oil, which is ideal because it incorporates an anti-frothing agent, has a minimal viscosity change with temperature and is almost incompressible.

Maintenance

The maintenance of a power-steering system, in addition to the work needed for normal steering, entails keeping the pump drive belt adjusted properly (and replacing it when necessary) and renewing the oil-filter element which is usually housed in the fluid reservoir. Normally the element is changed at intervals of 20,000 miles (32,000 km).

Adjustment

The adjustment of the rocker shaft of power-assisted steering boxes is generally carried out in the same way as for non-assisted types, that is, with the car jacked up and the steering at or near the straight-ahead position while rocking the steering wheel. When the steering begins to tighten up, back off the adjustment until it is free. Then lock it. On Burman power-steering units found on some Mk I and Mk II Jaguars there were shims under the adjusting screw. In this case, the shims were taken out, one by one, and the screw retightened until the steering began to run tight. Then the screw was removed, a 0.005 in. (0.125 mm) shim fitted and the screw replaced.

On Range Rover power steering, the rocker-shaft screw is adjusted to give a free-play of $\frac{3}{8}$ in. (9 mm) at the steering wheel rim.

Fault diagnosis, repair and overhaul

Power-steering boxes, rack-and-pinion units and rams are generally reliable and long-lived, and I would advise you to consider overhaul only when there is concrete evidence that it is needed. If a fault develops it makes sense to identify its cause, but there is no point in rushing headlong into dismantling a rather complicated component unnecessarily.

Power-assisted steering faults can be considered under several headings:

1. Insufficient power assistance when parking
Taking the simpler causes first: a slack drive belt will slip

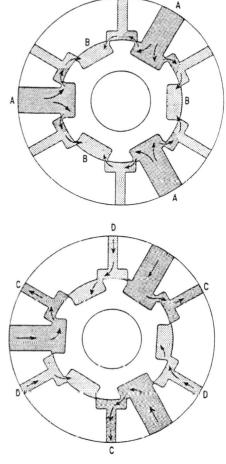

Fig. 6:6. A diagramatic cross-section of the Marles rotary valve used with rack-and-pinion pas and the Varamatic power-assisted steering box

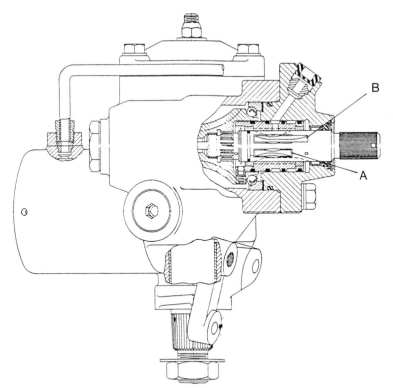

Fig. 6:7. A sectional view of the Marles valve in the Mk X Jaguar Varamatic steering system. Grooves A and B correspond to those in Fig. 6:6 (see text)

(perhaps accompanied by a shrieking noise) and reduce the pressure available. The belt is tensioned in the same way as a fan belt to give a total movement of about $\frac{1}{2}$ in. (13 mm).

A lack of fluid will lead to aeration and frothing in the system and loss of assistance. The system must be filled and bled to clear the air. In some cases all that is needed is to release the bleed screw (usually in the rocker-shaft cover) and, with the engine running, wait for clear air-free fluid to emerge before retightening it. *Don't raise the engine speed above idling or turn the wheel while this is going on.* On older units without a bleed screw the reservoir is filled with the engine idling. Then the engine speed is raised to about 1000 rpm and the wheels turned from lock to lock several times to clear the air. Whatever the type, you should ascertain the cause of the fluid shortage. While leaking hoses might be the reason, or even a leak from the steering box/unit itself, you should not overlook the possibility of a choked filter which, in some cases, may force fluid out of the reservoir.

If the engine idle speed is below the recommended setting, then the pump speed and its pressure will be reduced. If it is necessary to increase engine speed above the normal idle to obtain adequate assistance for parking, the pump itself is suspect and its pressure at idling should be checked. The procedure recommended for the Range Rover can be taken as a general guide. An adaptor *of sufficient strength* and a pressure gauge reading to 2000 psi (138 bar) should be attached to the outlet line of the pump and the system bled of air. The pressure is checked with the steering on full lock; at idling it should be about 400 psi (28 bar) and at 1000 rpm it should be 850–950 psi (60–67 bar). With the engine idling and the steering straight ahead, the pressure should be approximately 100 psi (7 bar).

2. *Unsatisfactory handling on the road*
This can manifest itself as a lack of castoring action, that is, the car seems to need constant steering correction or to steer in a series of straight lines, or the steering may seem oversensitive and 'twitchy'. In the former case, the cause is tightness in the system, possibly at a steering idler or due to

Fig. 6:8. In this in-line reactive steering system the valve, controlled by the drop-arm, feeds oil to a servo cylinder mounted between the tie-rod of a three-piece track-rod assembly and a side member of the vehicle's structure

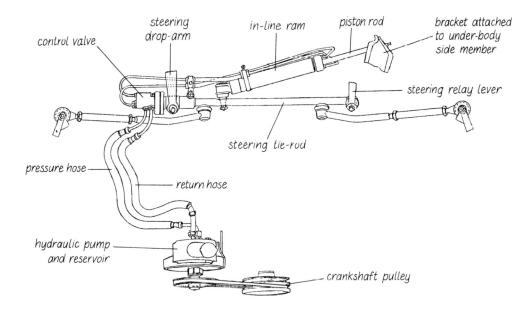

an overtightened rocker-shaft adjuster, while the latter is the result of a valve fault. It might be possible to renew the spring or springs controlling a spool valve to rectify the problem, but in the case of a torsion-bar-controlled rotary valve, the valve and worm assembly must be changed, which entails dismantling and rebuilding (or replacing) the steering unit.

3. Fluid leaks

Loss of fluid may be due to leaking hoses, gaskets or seals. Clean and dry the parts off, and then run the engine while you have a good look for the first signs of seepage. It might help to increase the engine speed to 750–1000 rpm, *but for not more than 30 seconds in any one minute*, turning the steering on full lock in each direction. This raises the fluid pressure and may amplify a leak. On the other hand, some leaks, especially from steering boxes, seem to show up better with the engine idling and the steering away from the extreme lock position.

4. Noisy operation

This is likely to be due to a pipe touching a panel, such as an inner wing, which amplifies the noise. Check carefully for this. On reactive systems it may be necessary to turn the steering from lock to lock since the pipes follow the movement of the servo cylinder (or ram). Noise is most likely to be evident if the steering is left in a full-lock position with the engine running—a practice that should be avoided.

Another source of noise is the relief valve inside the pump. Some improvement may be obtained by dismantling and cleaning the valve, lightly 'easing' any obvious high spots and lapping it in with crocus powder or jewellers' rouge, after which the valve and its bore must be cleaned thoroughly. If the pump is still noisy, it should be replaced.

5. Damaged castings

If the steering-box body is damaged, the castings cracked or cover-screw threads stripped, it is almost certainly due to a relief-valve fault giving rise to excessive pump pressure. Unless equipment is available to prove otherwise, the pump as well as the steering unit should be renewed.

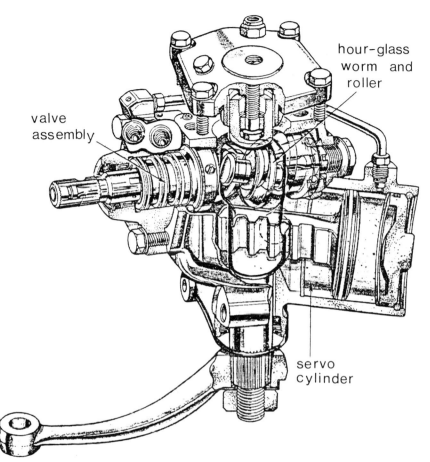

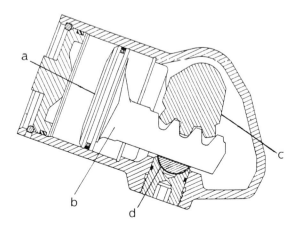

Above **Fig. 6:9.** This general view of the Varamatic assembly shows the valve mechanism, hour-glass worm and roller and the servo cylinder turning the rocker shaft through a rack

Left **Fig. 6:10.** This cross-section through the Varamatic servo cylinder shows piston (a), rack (b), toothed rocker shaft (c), and adjustable thrust button (d)

Repairs

Pumps
A certain amount of repair work can be done to a defective pump if a replacement is not available, though it may entail recourse to your local friendly machine shop. Try an engine-reconditioning specialist if you do not know where else to go.

Dismantling a Hoburn Eaton, vane or roller pump is well within the capability of the average amateur mechanic, provided you proceed carefully and note the order of assembly. The faults to look for are basically the same as those in engine oil pumps, that is, scoring of rotors and casings, excessive clearance between inner and outer rotors in the Hoburn Eaton type, and wear in the casing or the cover due to axial movement of the rotating parts. Additionally, valve faults can occur. The valve often acts as both a flow valve and a pressure-relief valve. It should be examined critically for any signs of sticking due to dirt or swarf becoming trapped between the valve and its bore, and for local damage such as burring or chipping. Sometimes burrs may be eased by careful attention with a *fine* slip stone (not the type used for sharpening carpentry tools), followed by lapping in with a very fine abrasive such as crocus powder, jewellers' rouge or perhaps one of the more easily obtainable burnishing compounds, such as T-Cut or Farecla G2, used by vehicle paint shops. After lapping, the valve, its bore and any adjacent holes must be *thoroughly* cleared of abrasive.

Not much can be done about worn vanes, rollers or rotors, but a scored end plate can be restored by surface grinding or, if you are unable to arrange this, by rubbing it on a sheet of *plate* glass covered with medium-grade emery-cloth. A machine shop might be able to mill out wear in the end of the casing, but the face on which the cover sits will have to be ground off to restore the correct dimension from the end of the bore.

The repairs listed above are suggestions of what might be done if replacements are not available; *if they are, use them.* If originality isn't everything, you might consider an alternative pump with similar characteristics from a more

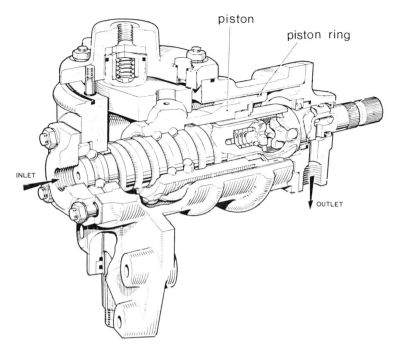

piston

piston ring

INLET

OUTLET

Fig. 6:11. Mk II Jaguar Burman
recirculating-ball pas system.
The nut forms the servo piston
(courtesy of Jaguar Cars Ltd)

recent vehicle. If so, you will have to sort out the associated problems of pulleys, belts and brackets.

Control valves

Only the spool valve lends itself to repair, but this should be considered only as a last resort. Like the pump valve, it may be chipped, burred or sticking due to the presence of dirt or swarf. If it is chipped on an edge controlling flow to or from the servo cylinder—forget it! You will *have* to find a replacement. Burrs can be dealt with as for pump valves.

Steering units and servo cylinders

No matter how experienced you are, there is *no* point in attempting to overhaul the steering unit and servo cylinder without a new set of seals and gaskets. You will also need some special tools but, in some cases, these could be made at home. In general, wear is not a major problem since the parts work in a clean environment, running in filtered fluid. Dealing with leaks may entail having hoses made up by a pipe specialist—they exist in most major towns. A leaking gasket, from something like a top cover, can be replaced by using the old one as a pattern for making a new one. In some cases, you might be able to replace the rocker-shaft oil seal without dismantling the unit.

At one time stripped cover threads were a problem, but if you take the box out it is possible to have them repaired with Helicoil thread inserts. The box need not be dismantled for this, but great care must be taken to prevent *any* swarf entering it.

If, after rocker-shaft adjustment, there still seems to be excess free movement you could try, with boxes like the Marles Varamatic (Jaguar Mk X), some judicious adjustment of the rocker-shaft damper pad. You will need to take the box out to do this. Beware of *any* significant tightening up as adjustment proceeds, backing it off as necessary.

In summary, if you have some experience, engineering skill, determination and access to resources, and there is no other way out, it might be possible to effect some repairs. Remember, however, that these components can be difficult to work on and must be sealed to withstand high fluid pressures. *If you can obtain a replacement unit, do so.*

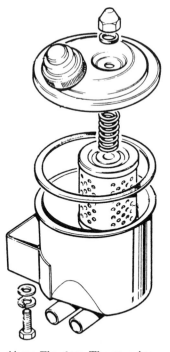

Above **Fig. 6:12. The steering reservoir filter should be changed every 20,000 miles as a blocked filter can cause oil to be forced out of the filler cap (courtesy of Land Rover Ltd)**

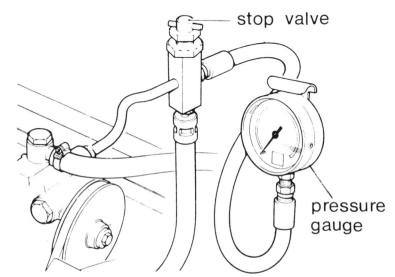

Right **Fig. 6:13. The set-up for pressure testing a pas system, in this case on a Rover (courtesy of Land Rover Ltd)**

Chapter 7 | Leaf-spring suspension

Up until 1940 the normal suspension arrangement for cars was beam axles front and rear suspended on leaf springs. Even the pioneering independent front suspensions, like that of the Standard Flying Eight, used this type of spring. Post-war, ifs by coil springs and wishbones, torsion bars or MacPherson struts became common, but the leaf spring remained the most popular rear suspension medium until the late 1960s. To this day it has not been totally eclipsed, so it is very probable that you will have to contend with leaf springs as part of your restoration work.

The most widely used leaf-spring arrangement was two springs per axle, each pivoted at the front and shackled at the rear to allow for extension as the spring flattened when the wheel hit a bump. Removal, overhaul and refitting of these springs is a straightforward and rewarding job, albeit somewhat 'physical' at times.

Spring removal

First jack the car well clear of the ground, making sure it is on a firm, flat surface. Chock the wheels of the other axle and support the car on stands placed under its chassis members or, in the case of unitary construction, a strong part of its underbody structure. Lower the jack until the springs are compressed no longer but the weight of the axle is still supported. If necessary, disconnect the dampers at this stage. Next release the U-bolts, or long bolts and retaining plates, that secure the axle to the centre of the spring, followed by the nuts on the shackle and pivot pins. Drive the pins out and lift the spring clear. Place a stand at each end of the axle as the springs are lifted out, and

Fig. 7:1. Stands should always be used when working under a car. Here they support prior to spring removal and there are more to support the axle when it comes free

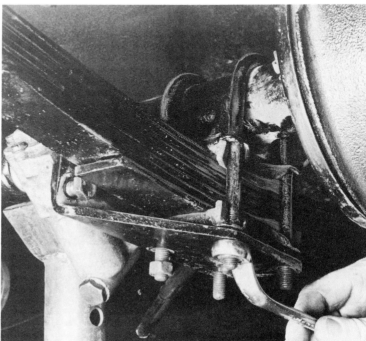

Fig. 7:2. The U-bolts are undone first and then the damper link should be released

another under the nose of the final-drive housing if it is a rear axle. This will prevent disturbance to the brake connections, pipes and cables, the drive at the rear, or steering linkage at the front.

Clean the spring, keeping an eye open for broken leaves and, possibly, a sheared centre bolt. Use a wire brush if the spring is mainly coated in dry road dirt; if it is greasy it should be washed. In some cases, springs are enclosed in gaiters, and these are likely to be greasy but free from grit.

In the absence of major breakages, you will have to decide whether your spring needs the attention of a specialist—a spring smith (difficult to find)—or whether you will have a go yourself. If the spring has flattened to the extent that it needs recambering, you should go to an expert, but don't jump to that conclusion too soon; some cars of the early post-war years, the Austin A40 Devons and Somersets in particular, had reverse-camber rear springs which bowed *upwards* when taking the weight of the unladen car.

To dismantle the spring, you have to release the clips,

Fig. 7:4. After removing the pivot pin, seen on the floor at bottom right, the spring can be lowered to the ground. Get help if it is a big spring

which may be riveted to the bottom leaf and 'cleated' over the top, or they may be retained by nuts and bolts. The centre bolt must be removed next, but note the following words of warning. It is possible to reassemble some leaves in the wrong order unless you mark them before taking them apart. Make a clear line with a file across the edges of the leaves on one side of the spring. For safety and to avoid leaves shooting all over the place, the energy contained in the spring must be released carefully. Clamp it firmly in a vice at a point near the centre bolt, remove the bolt and open the vice *slowly* to collect its leaves.

Inspection and overhaul

Inspect the dismantled spring for the condition of the leaves, of the centre bolt and of the bushes. Look for breaks

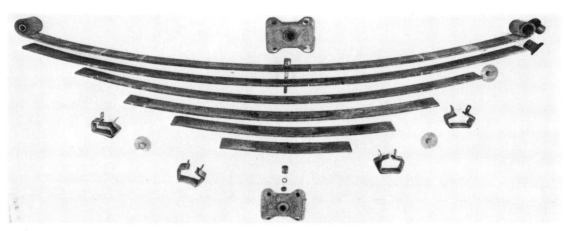

Above **Fig. 7:5. This dismantled leaf spring shows both top and bottom rubber-lined plates, centre bolt, dowel sleeve and nut, clips, inter-leaf plastic pads, plain unbonded rubber bushes (left) and a bonded-type rubber bush in the right-hand spring eye**

Left **Fig. 7:6. Metal bonded rubber bushes are often referred to by the trade names Silentbloc or Metalastik. The one shown has been partly fitted into the spring eye**

in the spring leaves and examine them critically for signs of wear—due to rubbing against their neighbours or a shortage of lubrication. The centre bolt should not be stretched, chafed or bent and its dowelling head should be in good condition.

Bushes may be of three different types: phosphor-bronze or, less commonly, brass—the pre-war norm—with hollow shackle pins having internal grease drillings and grooves; rubber bushes with thin steel cylinders bonded to their outer surfaces and smaller, but longer, steel cylinders in the centre—which appeared just before the war and were used increasingly afterwards—often referred to by the trade names Silentbloc or Metalastik; or unbonded rubber bushes—often two opposing 'half' bushes are used in each spring eye.

Fig. 7:7. Bushes can be fitted with a variety of methods including the vice and a steel block (shown), a drawing tool (see Fig. 8:11) or a drill press. Hammering them home is not a good idea

The drillings in metal bushes were seldom effective in carrying grease to all parts of the pins, so shackles became loose and rattled, allowing the car to move sideways on its springs. Frequent lubrication puts off the evil hour, but spring shackle maintenance and repair can be a bit of a pain. Many springs with metal bushes had shackles incorporating an adjusting nut for reducing endfloat on the bushes. Few cars since the 1940s have used metal bushes, and if replacements are required you will almost certainly need to have them made. They are driven or pressed into the spring eye using a solid punch above and a tube with a slightly larger internal diameter than the spring eye below. The bores of the bushes will need reaming to size after installation.

The bonded Silentbloc or Metalastik bush is probably the most difficult to change because its thin steel outer shell, originally an interference fit in the eye, can rust and be very difficult to move. When using a press or a hammer to remove these, the diameter of the punch should be just under that of the bush's outer shell. If all else fails, you may find you have to burn out the rubber with a welding torch or a blowtorch and saw through the metal shell to get it out. Wear a sprayer's respirator; the fumes from burning rubber are very pungent. The inner steel tube used in these composite bushes is longer than the outer. It is clamped by the shackle plates so that there is no free movement, only torsional deflection of the rubber. To avoid unnecessary torsional stress on the rubber, the nuts clamping the side plates should not be tightened until the vehicle is standing on a level surface with its weight on its wheels.

Unbonded rubber bushes are prone to wear but they are cheap and normally easy to change by prising them out of their mountings and pushing in the replacements.

Reassembly of the spring is more or less a reversal of the dismantling procedure. Lift the spring into place—unless it is a small one, get some help. Fit the pivot pin first, then attach the rear shackle loosely to the chassis. Jack the axle and locate the centre bolt head in its dowel hole. Carry on lifting until the lower shackle pin can be fitted. All that remains is to fit the U-bolts, or retaining bolts and plate, and the nuts to the shackle pins, tighten them up and connect the dampers. If the rear shackle is U-shaped or has its pins welded to the plate on one side, the shackle pins are slid into both the chassis bush and the spring eye after the spring has been jacked into place. Springs fixed below the axle will also need a slightly different technique. Having located the centre bolt, the U-bolts will have to be fitted and their nuts tightened lightly to retain the spring before jacking the axle to fit the shackled end. In a few cases a 'spreader' or 'stretcher' may be needed to attach the shackled end. After about 50 miles of running, retighten the U-bolts as the leaves may have bedded in or settled a little.

Above **Fig. 7:8. These simple, non-bonded bushes are commonly used in damper and steering linkages as well as spring eyes**

Below **Fig. 7:9. A Mk II Jaguar cantilever leaf-spring arrangement (courtesy of Jaguar Cars Ltd)**

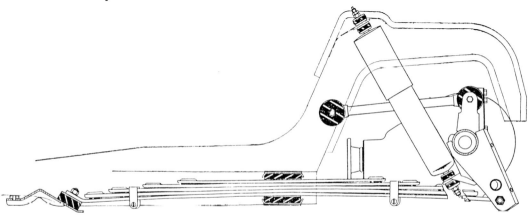

Variants and special procedures

The main variants are the cantilevered spring and the transverse spring. The former has been used to some extent and is usually of quarter-elliptic form, the motion of the axle being controlled by radius rods or an A-frame and torque-tube drive. In the Mk I and Mk II Jaguar saloons a semi-elliptic spring was used with the axle cantilevered at one end (i.e. hung where the shackle would otherwise be), the centre clamped to the frame and the other end bearing on a reaction pad. The Austin Seven of the 1920s and 1930s had a cantilevered quarter-elliptic at the rear, as did its latter-day relative the 'Frog Eye' Sprite. At the front, the Austin Seven featured a transverse semi-elliptic, an arrangement used by Ford for many years.

The removal of a quarter-elliptic spring is very easy; it is detached from the axle by knocking out a pin and released from the chassis section by unbolting it. The Jaguar system is a little more complex. The car is jacked up and supported on stands forward of the spring's front mounting point. Next the force on the spring's centre mounting is relieved by using a bottle jack under the spring eye. Then the centre clamping plate can be removed and the nut released from the spring-eye bolt, which is driven out. When refitting, the spring and its rubber mount are offered up into position and the bolts, centre plate and eye bolt fitted *but*

Fig. 7:10. Pre-war Austin Sevens and other cars had transverse leaf springs at the front and in this photograph the cantilevered rears can also just be seen

Above left **Fig. 7:11. Radius arms, such as these fitted to a Triumph Spitfire, are used to control transverse-leaf-spring suspension and one must make sure there is sound attachment between the front pivot and its outrigger**

Above **Fig. 7:12. This plate, behind the seats on a Triumph Spitfire, has to be removed to enable the spring/final-drive-housing retaining nuts to be undone. Some studs may also need to be removed**

not tightened. Then the car is lowered to the ground, bounced lightly so that the rubber parts assume their normal position, and the nuts are tightened with the weight of the vehicle resting on its wheels.

Transverse springs generally need a spreader for their removal and replacement. The rear spring is curved on Fords with this arrangement, so the spreader needs a

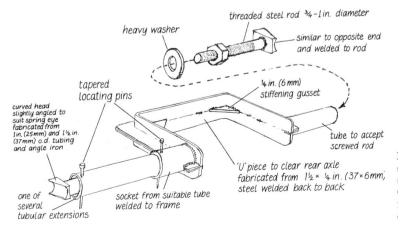

heavy washer

threaded steel rod ¾–1 in. diameter

similar to opposite end and welded to rod

tapered locating pins

¼ in. (6mm) stiffening gusset

curved head slightly angled to suit spring eye fabricated from 1 in. (25mm) and 1½ in. (37mm) o.d. tubing and angle iron

tube to accept screwed rod

one of several tubular extensions

socket from suitable tube welded to frame

'U' piece to clear rear axle fabricated from 1½ × ¼ in. (37×6mm) steel welded back to back

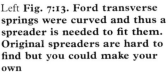

Left **Fig. 7:13. Ford transverse springs were curved and thus a spreader is needed to fit them. Original spreaders are hard to find but you could make your own**

Fig. 7:14. The spring can be drawn out sideways after removal of the eye bolts and dampers. Earlier, Mk I, II and III, models would also need the brake lines and propeller shaft to be disconnected

strong U-shaped section in the centre to clear the final-drive casing. J. W. Pickavant used to manufacture a very efficient tool for this purpose. Finding one for sale today would be difficult, but devising and manufacturing one might be an interesting job for the enthusiast with welding gear. A further point about Ford springs is that their metal-bonded rubber bushes had squared extensions to the integral through-bolts. When fitting these bushes, be certain to align the square shafts with the positions assumed by the shackle side plates when the spring is fitted.

The Triumph Spitfire employed a transverse leaf spring with independent rear suspension. On early models (Mks I, II and III) it was necessary to remove the propeller shaft and the flexible rear-brake pipes before freeing the spring. On the later Mk IV and 1500, the spring can be removed after taking off the dampers, relieving the load on the pins at the spring eyes, releasing these and driving them out. Then, after removing a cover inside the car, the nuts holding the spring to the final-drive housing can be unscrewed. However, before the spring is free, its studs must be extracted from the housing, after which it can be drawn out from the side of the vehicle. Refitting is basically a reversal of the removal procedure, taking account of the following points:

1. The spring clips marked 'front' must be towards the front of the car. The ground edge of the master leaf should also be to the front.
2. Tighten the bolts through the vertical links and spring eyes with the car standing on its wheels.
3. Use a sealant when refitting the floor panel to keep out water.

An alternative to the swinging shackle, which allows spring articulation and extension, was to use a circular block with a slot in it to take the spring, the block being free to move in its chassis mounting. This system works well if adequately lubricated. On dismantling, the spring can be slid from the block.

The system's dampers should be tested as described in chapter 3. If they are lever dampers of the vane or piston type, topping them up with a suitable oil may return them to serviceability.

Chapter 8 | Coil-spring suspension

Coil springs have been the most popular front suspension medium since the first post-war cars began to appear and, more recently, have become increasingly popular for rear suspension. Owing to the wide variety of layouts used, it is not possible to give specific advice on more than a few types representing some of the more popular arrangements.

Probably the most popular coil-spring system, albeit with many variants, is the 'double-wishbone' type. Next in popularity is the MacPherson strut arrangement pioneered by Ford but later adopted by Triumph, Rootes, BMW and many others. Less common applications are the trailing-link system used on some early post-war Aston Martins, the Rover knee-action linkage with its horizontal front spring, and Citroën's interconnected system operated through bell cranks and found on their twin-cylinder cars.

For three of the cars with double-wishbone suspension considered in this chapter, work on the springs, pivots, linkages, etc., can be done with the suspension cross-member still in the car, or the entire assembly can be taken off. While it is off, it can be cleaned, examined for rust damage (pretty unlikely), painted and rebuilt, perhaps leaving some final adjustments to do *in situ*.

I would recommend taking the cross-member off in the case of the Sunbeam Alpine and Jaguar Mk II. After disconnecting the brakes and steering of the former, unscrewing four vertical bolts through the chassis legs and four more transverse bolts under the wings will release the assembly. On the Jaguar, the steering shaft, brake pipes and anti-roll bar must be disconnected before releasing the six retaining bolts (one on each side through the chassis

Above **Fig. 8:1.** This coil-and-wishbone independent front suspension (ifs) from a Mk II Jaguar can be removed complete with its steering box after disconnecting brake pipes, steering shaft and just six bolts

Right **Fig. 8:2.** Ford and other manufacturers use this type of MacPherson strut. Note that the coil-spring compressors should be mounted diametrically. Note also the position of the top bearing and nut, stub axle, steering arm and, furthest from the camera, the ball pin for the track-control arms

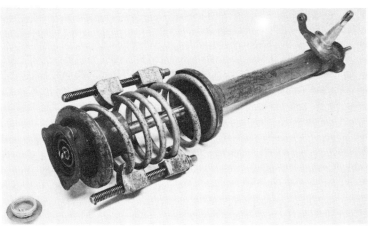

legs and two on each side at the front). However, if the work is being carried out on an MGB, it might be more convenient, from the point of view of handling the spring, to do the job on the car.

Springs

If coil springs are released suddenly, they can be *very dangerous*, so when being compressed or released they must be kept under control. There are various ways in

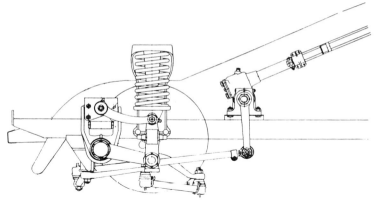

Left **Fig. 8:3. The stub axle of this Aston Martin DB 2/4 is mounted on a carrier guided by two trailing links, the upper one being the damper arm. The lower end of the spring bears on the stub-axle carrier, the upper in a cast-aluminium turret (courtesy of Aston Martin Lagonda Ltd)**

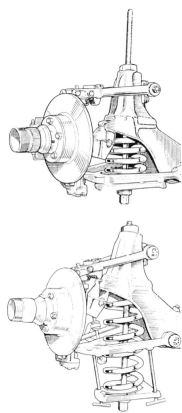

which this can be done, one of which is to use clamps that engage with the coils and can be tightened with spanners to compress the spring and slackened to release it. At least two of these are needed for each spring and they must be in good condition, the nuts running freely on their threads so there is no tendency for the clamping hooks to turn during tightening or releasing and disengage from the coils. The hooked part of the clamp should be in good condition and the threaded rods should not be bent. Another method is to jack the suspension, compressing the spring, and use fixed-length, flat metal clamps to retain the spring in its compressed state. The clamps can be made safer by fitting a hoop around them to prevent them slipping off. I am not very keen on this method since it entails storing the spring in its compressed and potentially dangerous condition.

A number of cars with double-wishbone systems had a coil spring which was inserted through a large hole in the lower wishbone and secured by a small plate bolted into place. In some instances, the damper fits inside the spring and is easily removed without disturbing it. Some springs installed in this way can be removed safely with the aid of two fully-threaded 'slave' bolts perhaps 4–6 in. (100–150 mm) long. When this technique is used on some cars (such as the Austin A30), it is recommended that the upper link (also forming the damper arm) should be held about $1\frac{1}{8}$ in. (28 mm) above the upper face of the spring abutment. This avoids damaging the bump stop. The slave bolts are substituted for two diametrically-opposed original short

Top **Fig. 8:4. Here is a compressor fitted to a Mk II Jaguar prior to front spring removal (courtesy of Jaguar Cars ltd)**

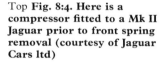

Above **Fig. 8:5. When refitting the Jaguar spring, long threaded pilot studs guide the spring plate into position (courtesy of Jaguar Cars Ltd)**

Fig. 8:6. To separate the Spitfire spring from the damper the spring must be compressed with clamps before undoing the lock nut, the nut on the central stud and the top plate

bolts. Then the two remaining original bolts are undone and removed, after which the slave bolts can each be unscrewed a little at a time until the spring is released and comes away with its lower plate.

On some other coil-and-wishbone arrangements, such as those of Mk I and Mk II Jaguar saloons, Sunbeam Alpines and Rapiers and their humbler cousins, the Gazelle, Minx and Husky, a long, stout through-bolt is used to hold the spring while the lower plate is disconnected. Then the bolt is unscrewed, lowering the spring. Replacing the spring is a reversal of the above, except that the use of long guide pins to align the spring-plate holes is advised on the Jaguar.

On the Triumph Spitfire and its close relations, the GT6, Vitesse and Herald, the combined spring and damper can be removed as a single unit after disconnecting the anti-roll bar and supporting the car with its weight off the springs. All that is necessary is to release three bolts at the top of the spring and a single cross-pin passing through the damper eye below. With the unit off the car, spring clamps or a compressor may be used to take the pressure off the upper spring plate (or pan) so that the bolt attaching it to the damper can be unscrewed. Finally, the spring can be gradually and carefully released to separate the units.

When working on the coil-and-wishbone suspension of the MGB, it is not very practical to remove the spring at the beginning of the job. On the other hand, with reasonable care, a flat working surface and a good trolley jack, this task can be handled without special tools. After the car has been supported on stands, the road wheel is removed together with its caliper (laid to one side so that its flexible pipe is not strained), hub and mudshield. The anti-roll bar is disconnected. Then a trolley jack is placed under the spring pan between the two lower-wishbone arms so that its arm swings in a similar arc to that of the wishbone. The jack is raised sufficiently to just take the load of the spring off its bump stops. After releasing the upper pivot pin that passes through the damper arms and slackening the bolt where these two come together, the pivot pin can be drifted out. *Be careful*; at this stage the full force of the spring is on

the jack, which should be lowered gently to release it.

Ford cars of the mid-1960s, such as the Mk I Cortina, had MacPherson strut suspension. Before removing one of these assemblies, fixed-length clips should be fitted over as many spring coils as possible with the car still on its wheels, and a safety hoop placed around the clips to keep them in place. With the car supported on an unsprung part of its structure, the road wheel, brake drum (if so equipped) and hub are removed from the stub axle as an assembly after unpinning and removing the wheel-bearing nut. The brake back plate should be removed and suspended so as not to tension its pipe. Then the track-control arm is released as is the track-rod-end ball pin. Three bolts are released from under the bonnet and the complete unit

Above left **Fig. 8:7. Removing a front spring unit from a Triumph Spitfire entails undoing three nuts and removing the lower damper eye bolt**

Above **Fig. 8:8. Removing the upper fulcrum pin during the dismantling of MGA suspension**

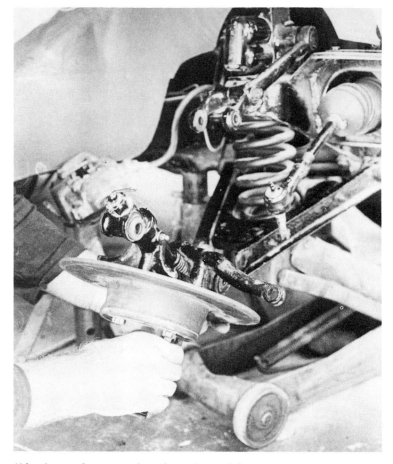

Fig. 8:9. After removing the
lower fulcrum pin, the swivel
and hub can be lifted clear

lifted out from under the wing. After unscrewing a self-
locking nut, you can remove the upper thrust bearing
followed by the upper spring seat. At this stage the spring
may be lifted off and, by using a suitable compressor, the
clips can be removed and the spring unloaded.

Replacement of pivot pins and bushes

There are many different types of pins and bushes. Early
bushes tended to be metal and later versions rubber or
plastic.

An early volume-production ifs using coil springs and
wishbones, that of the A40 Devon, had screwed bushes on
a threaded fulcrum pin. These were relatively trouble free.
The bushes were located on their arms, and the fulcrum in

the king pin, by cotter pins. With the arrival of the A30 in the early 1950s, a simpler and cheaper version emerged. At the outer end of the lower wishbone/spring pan (unceremoniously nicknamed 'the lavatory seat' by mechanics) was a threaded, double-diameter fulcrum that was screwed, not into separate bushes, but into the wishbone. After a few years' use and possibly neglected lubrication—the lubrication interval was 1000 miles (1600 km)—it was by no means uncommon to find them impossible to remove. The fulcrum was supposed to be unscrewed from the wishbone/pan using a screwdriver. More often than not, all efforts to do this were fruitless, the screwdriver slowly being destroyed by the hardened pin. The only way out was (and is) expensive: to replace the king pin, fulcrum and lower wishbone/pan. These parts are available for many cars (such as the Austin Healey Sprite) to this day.

If you are desperate, you might be able to salvage a good king pin from a 'dodgy' wishbone/pan by cutting, burning and grinding away most of the metal from the latter, then either paring away the shell of the smaller integral screwed

Fig. 8:10. The MGA suspension bears a family resemblance to this early A40 Devon. Note the metal screwed lower fulcrum bushes (a), the unusual half-moon cotter pins (b) [do not try to drive these out until the fulcrum pin has been removed], and the forged lower-wishbone arms (c). Though well engineered, this assembly was heavy and needed frequent lubrication and damper renewal

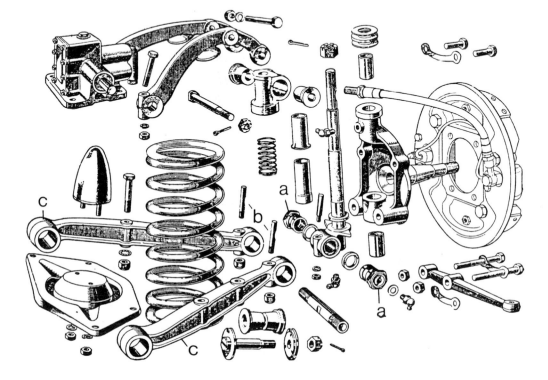

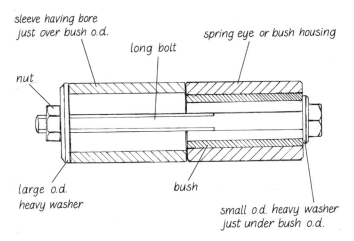

sleeve having bore
just over bush o.d.

long bolt

spring eye or bush housing

nut

large o.d.
heavy washer

bush

small o.d. heavy washer
just under bush o.d.

Fig. 8:11. There is a bush-drawing tool but many restorers prefer to use a vice or a press

bush from the fulcrum with a chisel or cutting off the fulcrum using the edge of a grinding disc. After doing this and driving out the cotter, you can drive the remains of the fulcrum from the king pin.

Another type of pin, in a similar layout, occurs on the MGB. This, too, is a frequent source of trouble (probably due to neglected lubrication). In this design the screwed fulcrum is replaced by a distance piece surrounding a pin and passing through a plain bush. Neglect causes the distance piece and pin to seize in the bush so that the latter moves in the wishbone ends, knocking out the holes. If the pin has seized in its distance piece, one of the arms must be removed to release the steering swivel. The remedy will be new arms, bush, pin and distance piece together with the minor bits that make up the sealing arrangements.

A similar seizure occurs at the bottom fulcrum on Triumphs. Here, the bushes are of plastic, so neglected lubrication cannot be blamed. The pin is surrounded by a distance piece to which it rusts, preventing it being driven out. If the spring/damper unit is taken out and the hub dismantled, you might find you can introduce a hacksaw blade, without a frame or handle, and saw the pin off on both sides, inside the channel. Then you are home and dry; you can lift out the swivel and drive out the pin and distance piece, picking out the remains of the bushes—unless the holes in the lower link are damaged. Reassembly is straightforward and obvious.

The fitting of simple rubber bushes can be made easier by polishing the holes or eyes into which they fit and smearing the bushes with a solution of water and hand cleaner (Swarfega or similar) or washing-up liquid.

If you have difficulty in fitting a metal-and-rubber bonded bush, polish the eye or hole with emery-cloth. Use a punch that is just under the diameter of the outer steel sleeve, backing the eye or hole with a piece of steel tubing slightly larger than the sleeve's outside diameter. Rather than drive the bush in with a hammer, it is better to push it in with a press or, as a substitute, a pillar drill stand or a large vice.

You can use a similar technique for all metal bushes, be they of brass, phosphor-bronze, or the steel-backed

Top left **Fig. 8:12. To remove the damper from this tired-looking Sunbeam Alpine one must first remove both nut and lock nut from the top . . .**

Above **Fig. 8:13. . . . followed by the two nuts at the bottom . . .**

Bottom left **Fig. 8:14. . . . after which the damper can be drawn out leaving the rest of the suspension undisturbed**

Above **Fig. 8:15. Removing the camber shims, indicated with a screwdriver, on this Mk II Jaguar increases positive camber**

Above right **Fig. 8:16. Positive castor on the Mk II Jaguar can be increased by transferring shims from the rear to the front of the upper ball-joint mounting**

variety. Sometimes a tool can be made up to 'draw' a bush in or out. This idea is popular in DIY manuals, but I have not had much success with this method when the bush is really tight. Fig. 8:11 shows the general idea.

Damper replacement

If a damper is faulty it must be replaced. Long-term there is not much point in topping up the few versions (lever types and early MacPherson struts) on which this is possible. (See chapter 3 for details of damper testing.)

On Jaguar and Rootes coil-spring layouts of the sort mentioned, the damper is fitted inside the spring. By unbolting it top and bottom, you can draw it out with ease (provided you have jacked the car high enough) and without disturbing the spring.

For BL coil-and-wishbone suspensions and their Austin, BMC, MG, etc., predecessors, proceed in the same way as when removing a spring. However, once the upper fulcrum pin has been removed, four bolts attaching the damper can be undone and it can be taken out. Unless you are fitting a replacement immediately, carry on and remove the spring. It is dangerous to leave it otherwise.

As has been said earlier, Triumph dampers are removed

with their springs, and the Ford MacPherson strut is a damper unit in itself.

Suspension linkage adjustment

Although some of the suspensions considered are, to some extent, adjustable, the steering geometry should have been set properly when the car left the factory and should not alter. If a check at a garage reveals a fault, it will indicate that accidental damage has occurred and gone uncorrected.

If you are a perfectionist, you might want to use any adjustment facility to bring the settings nearer the centre of their limits, especially if you are changing from cross-ply to radial tyres. On the Jaguar, for example, the camber setting is $\frac{1}{2}$ degree positive plus or minus $\frac{1}{2}$ degree, i.e. between zero degrees and 1 degree positive. If you found 1 degree on the nearside and zero degrees on the offside there would be a tendency, which might not be felt, for the steering to pull to the nearside. Obviously, it would be better to reset the camber to give $\frac{1}{2}$ degree positive on both sides. In general, the more 'precise' behaviour of radial tyres tends to accentuate steering-geometry faults due to suspension defects.

On the Jaguar and Sunbeam suspensions covered here the camber is adjustable by shims. In both cases the removal of shims increases positive camber. Shims in the Sunbeam span both mounting bolts, but on the Jaguar there is a separate shim for each bolt. When adjusting camber, it is important that shims of equal thickness are removed or added at each bolt, or an unwanted change of castor will occur. The Jaguar's suspension is also adjustable for castor by transferring shims from one side of the upper ball joint to the other.

Accident damage

Here we are not necessarily talking about the results of a crash; accidental damage can occur after a heavy 'kerbing' or hitting a bit of unmade road at speed, or even from careless jacking—some pressed-steel parts are of very light construction. As mentioned above, if the steering geometry is out, you should look for accidental damage. The problem is how? Everything on your car will either be

Fig. 8:17. Coil springs are not infallible as you can see by this broken unit on the rear of a Vauxhall Chevette

Fig. 8:18. The Chevette had typical 1970s small-car coilspring suspension with the axle located by trailing arms, antiroll bar, Panhard rod, and angled dampers. Drive is via a short torque-tube

covered by road dirt and rust or will have been cleaned and painted so that it all looks pretty much the same.

Minor damage to wishbones or the track-control arms of MacPherson strut suspensions, steering arms and stub axles is best diagnosed by comparison with known sound items. For most restorers, finding a sound pattern will be very difficult, but if one side of your car is wrong and the other is right, use parts from the good side which are mirror images of the suspect parts as comparisons. Fig. 8:21, taken from a Jaguar manual, shows some measurements that could easily be established and checked from one side to the other. Bear in mind that the nearside is likely to have suffered more from kerbing than the offside.

If the steering and suspension linkage seems okay, it is possible that the chassis or bodyshell has been damaged and that, perhaps, during a previous accident repair, this has gone unnoticed. If you suspect that this is the case, a drop test should be carried out to assess chassis alignment or, better still, the bodyshell should be checked using a jig and the proper brackets if they are available. The former can be done on a complete car in running order and entails dropping plumb lines from datum points to the floor, drawing diagonals and checking that their intersections are in line. The latter requires taking a stripped or partially-stripped bodyshell to a specialist vehicle repairer—difficult. If you have any suspicions at all from ripples in the structure near suspension mounting points, paint damage or whatever, making card templates on the good side of the car and comparing them with the other might just point the way to what is wrong.

Unusual coil-spring applications

Rover

The P6 models had a complex front suspension, operating through a bell crank, which turned the vertical suspension travel through 90 degrees so that the spring reaction was taken on the central body cage. The replacement of bushes and ball joints, etc., follows conventional lines as discussed in this chapter and in chapters 4 and 7. Much of the linkage can be overhauled without taking out or compressing the spring.

If you do need to take the spring off, unbolt the front wing so that you can see what you are doing. You will need some assistants to bear down on the front of the car while you insert three special rods in the 'pan' at the forward end of the spring, passing them through slots in the back and turning them through 90 degrees to lock the spring in the compressed state. It will also be necessary to take off the upper steering swivel and the top-link mounting plate as well as disconnecting the anti-roll bar and damper.

Aston Martin DB 2, 2/4 and Mk III

These cars have an unusual double trailing-link system which earned the cars an enviable reputation for roadholding and handling. Each of the two main links turns on a hollow shaft mounted between widely-spaced bearings (a needle-roller bearing at the outboard end and a ball race inboard). These bearings are housed in aluminium castings bolted to the chassis side rails. The housings are held together by a third which carries the steering relay lever and encloses an anti-roll torsion bar. This bar is splined into the outer ends of the shafts referred to above. The three castings form an assembly, excluding dirt and containing oil to lubricate the moving parts.

To allow removal and dismantling of the suspension, the car should be lifted and placed on stands, *but do not jack these cars on the aluminium suspension housing*. Remove the road wheels and hub and brake assemblies, tying up the latter to avoid disturbing their hydraulic brake pipes. Take

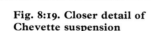

Fig. 8:19. Closer detail of
Chevette suspension

the load from the springs by removing the upper links and
undo the bump stop which is inside the spring, allowing it
to drop down. The spring can be prised from its housing or
just lifted off if a spring compressor is used. Remove the
domed nut from the main trailing link and drive it off its
tapered shaft from the opposite side of the vehicle, using a
solid bar and a hammer. After removing the three-piece
suspension casting, mark its flanges for correct reassembly
and unbolt it at both ends of the centre section. At this
stage the housing shafts, bearings and anti-roll bar can be
examined. Since these units were so well engineered, it is
likely that everything will be in good order. Bearings are
most likely to be at fault, but they will probably be
obtainable from a bearing specialist.

Reassembly is basically a reversal of the dismantling
procedure. Again, the treatment of ball pins, bushes, etc.,
follows conventional lines, but note that the outer needle
bearing is fitted *after* the hollow shaft. Don't forget to fill
the casting with oil.

Coil springs for rear suspension

Beam axles

A popular arrangement in the late 1960s and 1970s, which
began to eclipse the traditional semi-elliptic springs, was to
use coil springs with a live beam axle controlled by two
trailing links and a transverse Panhard rod. By leaning the
dampers inwards, they assist in the lateral location of the
axle. In the example shown in Figs. 8:18 and 8:19, the
dampers are easily removed by disconnecting their top
mountings and telescoping them downwards, after which
the lower nuts are undone and they are pulled off their
pins. Spring removal is also easy. In many cases, with the
dampers released at one end (usually the top), the links will
drop far enough for the spring to be removed without
needing a compressor. The type shown needs just a little
help from spring clamps when replacing the springs. It is
important to keep the link and Panhard rod bushes in good
order, otherwise handling will be impaired.

De Dion axles

This design is not at all common, but it has been in use

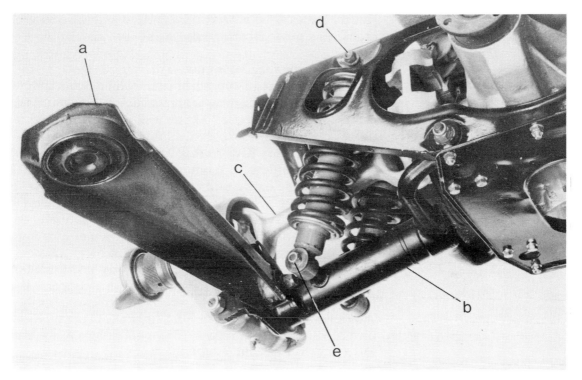

Fig. 8:20. Jaguar E type irs showing trailing radius arms (a), lower link (b), and the drive shaft which forms the upper link (c). By removing two bolts (d) and nuts (e), the coil-overs can be removed (courtesy of Jaguar Cars Ltd)

since the 'dawn' of motoring. The arrangement links the two rear wheels by an axle beam (usually tubular) and has a chassis-mounted final drive with two universally-jointed half shafts. It is claimed to combine the advantages of both the beam axle and independent rear suspension in that unsprung weight is kept low with minimal variation in track and wheelbase.

In the Rover P6 layout, spring changing is very easy after jacking and supporting the rear of the car so that the wheels are 1 ft (300 mm) or so from the ground. A jack is placed under the rear of the bottom link, the damper disconnected at its lower end, the bolt which attaches the link to the hub carrier removed and the jack lowered to allow the spring to be lifted out. On replacement, care should be taken to locate the spring properly at top and bottom and to ensure that any distance pieces are in place. The bolt attaching the link to the hub carrier should not be tightened until the car is standing on its wheels. The suspension height for P6

Rovers is measured between the ground and the centre of the chassis pivot for the upper (rear) link.

Independent rear suspension

Jaguar Mk X E and S types had an irs which featured four coil springs installed around dampers and in which the half shafts formed the upper links as well as transmitting the drive. It was built up as an assembly with the final drive unit and inboard disc brakes in a heavy pressed-steel 'cage'. If a significant amount of work is to be done, as in a restoration, the entire unit can be taken out, but bear in mind that it is a big, heavy lump. After removing the exhaust pipes to clear the way and putting stands under the car ahead of the radius-arm mountings, a jack is placed under the centre mounting plate with a block of wood about 9 in. (225 mm) square and 1 in. (25 mm) thick in between to prevent local damage. The jack supports the unit while the bolts at the front and rear rubber mountings, the anti-roll bar, radius-arm front ends, the brake pipe and propeller shaft are released. You will need a couple of assistants to guide and control the assembly as you lower it to the floor.

One of the jobs that can be done with the Jaguar suspension unit *in situ* is the replacement of the spring-and-damper units, although it is much more convenient to do it with the unit out of the car and placed on a low bench. The pin holding the lower ends of the dampers is simply undone and, with the wishbone supported, driven out. Taking out the nut and bolt at the top releases each damper from the cage. You will need some sort of spring compressor to unload the spring so that the collets can be removed from the dampers and the springs taken off. Use a substantial press, compressor or clamps—or get someone to do it for you—*don't improvise*. Reverse the procedure for reassembly.

The inner end of the wishbone pivots on needle-roller bearings and the outer is carried on tapered-roller bearings at the hub carrier. When tapping out the wishbone spindles follow through with a dummy shaft to keep the bits and pieces aligned—there are a lot of small circular parts at the inner end. At the outer end be sure to collect any shims and not to lose the oil-seal tracks. Shims must be kept in their correct positions.

When restoring one of these units be critical of the rubber bushes at the ends of the radius arms and the dampers. If you are not absolutely satisfied that they are as good as new, replace them together with the rubber mountings for the whole assembly.

The rear wheels should have a small negative camber at the mid-point of suspension travel. This is adjusted by shims at the inner end of the drive shafts between the universal joint and the brake disc; one shim alters the camber by about $\frac{1}{4}$ degree.

There are many other irs layouts with coil springs. Following the general rules provided for checking dampers, dealing with tapers, replacing bushes, measuring suspension heights and, above all, dealing sensibly with springs, the amateur mechanic should be able to devise ways of coping with them.

Fig. 8:21. If steering or suspension components are suspected of having suffered accident damage, compare them with either the manufacturers' drawings or the other side of the car if undamaged

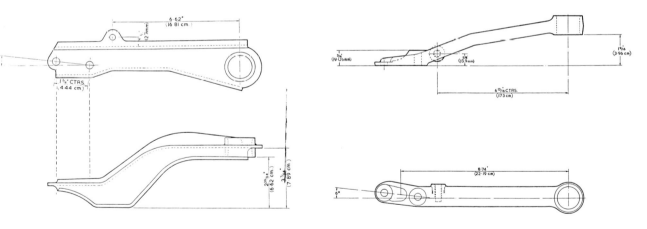

Upper Wishbone Lever (Pressed steel type).

Upper Wishbone Lever (Forged type).

Chapter 9 | Torsion-bar suspension

Fig. 9:1. By undoing the retainer plate and turning the vertical screw (bottom left) the height of the front of this Riley RM with torsion-bar suspension can be adjusted

Once challenging coil springs as a medium for front suspension, the torsion bar seems to have lost popularity, but many classic cars use it, two examples being the Morris Minor and the Jaguar E type.

Nothing more needs to be said about dealing with ball pins, bushes or tapers since they have been covered in previous chapters. Bear in mind, too, the points made in chapter 3 about torsion bars being loaded and the need to replace them on the correct side of the car. There are a number of features common to all torsion-bar suspensions, and this chapter will deal with three typical examples, showing how to change and adjust the torsion bars.

The torsion-bar adjustment on Riley RM cars is by a threaded adjuster connected by a short arm to the torsion bar and mounted on a bracket attached to a cross-member running under the gearbox bell housing. Turning the adjusting screw clockwise raises the body and vice versa, but it is important that the height is *not* increased with the weight of the car on the wheels. Reducing the height with the weight on the wheels is allowed, however.

Before adjusting the suspension, the tyre pressures should be equalized at 24 psi (1.7 bar). After making the adjustment, the car should be bounced a few times and rolled backwards and forwards slightly to settle the suspension before checking the height. The setting is correct when the vertical distance between a flat floor and the centre of the lower wishbone's outer swivel is $1\frac{1}{2}$ in. (38 mm) less than the vertical distance between the floor and the centre of the wishbone's inner swivel.

To change a Riley torsion bar, the car should be jacked

up and supported well clear of the floor on stands at the front. The height adjuster is backed off a little and, after taking off a rubber cap at the front and disconnecting the retainer plate at the rear adjuster, the bar can be driven out forwards or backwards, whichever is more convenient. When fitting a replacement bar the adjuster must be backed right off and a helper should bear down slightly on the wheel to assist in starting the bar's splines. Then the bar can be driven in, the retainer plate reassembled and the height set as described.

The E type Jaguar has torsion bars at the front and is an example of a car with which care must be taken when jacking and supporting the chassis. A piece of hard wood should be cut to fit inside the chassis front cross-member to spread the load. When the car has been lifted, supporting axle stands should be placed *under the lower-wishbone-pivot support bracket, not the frame tubes.* Care should also be taken not to damage the upper-wishbone ball joint by allowing the lower wishbone to drop any further than its normal rebound position—an important point if the damper is removed.

With a full tank of petrol, normal oil and water levels, the front tyres at 23 psi (1.62 bar) and the rear tyres at 25 psi (1.76 bar), the centre of the lower wishbone's inner pivot should be $8\frac{3}{4}$ in. plus or minus $\frac{1}{4}$ in. (222 mm plus or minus

Below left **Fig. 9:2.** It is advisable to use a shaped block of wood when jacking. This Jaguar E type is supported under the inner wishbone pivot

Below **Fig. 9:3.** E type castor can be adjusted by releasing the clamps and turning the screwed wishbone pivot

Above **Fig. 9:4.** E type camber can be adjusted by adding or subtracting shims from beneath the pivots of the upper wishbone. Adding shims increases positive camber

Right **Fig. 9:5.** When setting the height of an E type the upper wishbones, anti-roll bar and steering tie-rod ball pin all need to be disconnected. With the damper removed this setting gauge can be installed

6 mm) from the ground.

Adjustment requires some preliminary work. First, a setting gauge must be made from an $18\frac{13}{16}$ in. (477.8 mm) length of $1 \times \frac{1}{4}$ in. (25 × 6 mm) mild-steel bar. This should have two holes drilled in it at $17\frac{13}{16}$ in. (452.5 mm) centres; one should be drilled $\frac{1}{2}$ in. (13 mm) from the end of the bar and be $\frac{29}{64}$ in. (11.5 mm) in diameter, the other should be $\frac{41}{64}$ in. (16.2 mm) in diameter.

The upper-wishbone ball joint should be disconnected along with the steering track-rod ball pin and the anti-roll bar. Then the nuts retaining the lower-wishbone rubber mountings are unpinned and slackened. With a jack under the suspension near the lower damper mounting, the damper is removed, as are the two bolts holding the torsion-bar rear adjuster bracket to the vehicle's frame. After adjusting the height of the lower wishbone with the jack, the setting gauge is bolted to the frame and the wishbone in place of the damper. The holes in the torsion-bar bracket should align with those in the frame. If they don't, ease the bracket from its splines, and rotate it and refit it so that they do. Since one end of the bar has 25 splines and the other 24, adjustment to $\frac{1}{600}$ turn is possible. For this, however, the front end of the bar must be disconnected, which entails removing its locking bolt and sliding the bar back. If only the back end is freed, adjustment is by intervals of $\frac{1}{25}$ turn.

If the torsion bar is freed at both ends, it can be removed by first pushing it backwards and then downwards and forwards. After carrying out adjustment and refitting the bolts to the rear torsion-bar bracket, together with the clamp bolt at the front, the gauge can be removed, the suspension lifted a little on the jack and the damper upper ball joint and track-rod ball joint fitted. Leave the nuts on the damper and the lower wishbone finger-tight. Lower the car to the ground, push it forward about 4 ft (1.2 m) and check the height. If it is correct (as it should be) tighten the nuts on the damper and lower pivot, securing the latter with a split pin.

The E type front suspension is adjustable for both castor and camber. Castor is adjusted by unlocking and rotating the upper pivot of the top wishbone, thus moving the

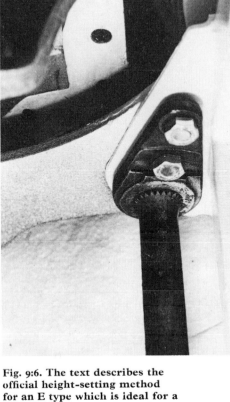

Fig. 9:6. The text describes the official height-setting method for an E type which is ideal for a completely assembled car, but during assembly it may be easier to have the gauge in position and this setting arm bolted up. One can then offer up both sets of splines, just starting the rears, until they match upon which the bar can be driven home and the locating bolt fitted

Fig. 9:7. Before removing the torsion bar on this Riley RM one must remove the rubber cap (see text)

upper ball joint forward to decrease castor or backward to increase it. Camber is adjusted with shims behind the upper-wishbone inner pivot. Some fairly simple, special tools are needed for these jobs, but they could be made by the amateur restorer. However, garage equipment will be needed to measure the angles.

When changing a Morris Minor torsion bar, the front suspension arm should be jacked near its outer end. After removal of the road wheel and the angled tie-bar, the pressed-steel front half of the suspension arm is removed, as is the link pin at the pivot of the lower trunnion. Then the car should be lowered on to an axle stand to unload the

Above **Fig. 9:8.** The front part of the lower suspension arm of this Morris Minor being removed after undoing the tie-rod and moving away the lower trunnion. Note forked bolt for the tie-rod in the mechanic's right hand

Left **Fig. 9:9.** During assembly the rear half of the lower arm can be fitted on to the bar after it has been threaded through the lever (left) and the rear cross-member

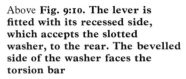

Above **Fig. 9:10. The lever is fitted with its recessed side, which accepts the slotted washer, to the rear. The bevelled side of the washer faces the torsion bar**

torsion bar. Next remove the nut from the end of the torsion bar at the cross-member under the car, followed by the nut and bolt holding the lever to the cross-member. Slide the lever forward off its splines, collecting the slotted washer, and disengage the torsion-bar splines from the suspension arm. Pull the bar clear.

When refitting the bar, thread it through the lever (recessed side to the rear) and the cross-member. Engage the front of the bar in the suspension arm. Jack the rear half of the suspension arm so that its inner pivot is $5\frac{5}{8}$ in. (143 mm) higher than the outer one. Slide the lever at the rear over the splines so that its eye aligns with the slot in the cross-member. Insert the slotted washer, making sure that it registers with the recess in the lever. Replace the nut and washer on to the rear of the bar, ensuring that its smaller diameter registers with the hole in the frame. Fit the adjuster plate behind the torsion bar, using whichever hole is in alignment. Refit the trunnion to the rear half of the suspension arm and replace the front half of the arm, the tie-bar and the road wheel. With the weight of the car on the wheels, the inner pivot should be $1\frac{5}{8}$ in. (41 mm) above the outer one.

Right **Fig. 9:11. With the lever arm set so that its inner pivot is $5\frac{5}{8}$ in. (143 mm) higher than the outer one and the bar engaged with it, the lever is slid over the rear splines and aligned with the curved slot in the cross-member. The adjustment plate is slid under the lever and the bolt fitted. Its nut and that which screws on to the end of the torsion bar are fitted and tightened**

Chapter 10 | Rubber/hydraulic suspension

This chapter will consider the BMC/BL suspension introduced on the Mini and featured in modified form on its stablemates. Citroën, of course, are well known for the advanced hydraulic suspension systems featured on their larger cars but, although there is a dedicated band of Citroën enthusiasts, in general their appeal to restorers is limited. In view of this and the complexity of the systems, they will not be considered here.

The BMC suspension came in three forms: rubber, Hydrolastic and Hydragas. The last was introduced in the 1970s on a number of cars which so far have failed to achieve any sort of 'classic' or 'collectable' status. Originally, the cars had a double-link arrangement at the front with a rubber 'spring' above the upper arm, while at the rear a trailing radius arm operated a horizontal spring through a bell crank. When the Hydrolastic system was introduced, hydraulic 'displacers' replaced the rubber springs.

Rubber suspension

For a number of jobs on rubber suspension at the front of the car, it is essential to compress the spring. On the Mini, this is done with a special tool (Leyland part number 18G 574B). However, the tool can be made as described in chapter 4, which also explains its use. Compression of the rubber spring allows removal or *in situ* adjustment of the upper and lower steering/suspension ball swivels, the replacement of the strut and ball joint connecting the spring to the upper arm, the removal and refitting of the upper arm, and the replacement of the spring unit. When

Fig. 10:1. This rubber front 'spring' on a Mini is being compressed with a DIY tool

tackling the first of these jobs, compressing the spring will make releasing the swivel ball-pin tapers much easier, especially if the lower one is removed first. (See chapter 4 for swivel adjustment.)

The strut and its ball-and-socket connection are simply pulled out of the unit for renewal, but the plastic socket cup must be prised out. The ball fits into the cup which pushes into the top of the arm and is sealed by a gaiter. After taking out the strut, you might wish to go further and remove the upper link, perhaps to replace its needle-roller bearings. This is done by removing the nut and washer from each end of the shaft, followed by the front thrust collar and plate, pushing the shaft forward and removing the rear thrust washer and seal. Then the link can be manoeuvred out. The word 'manoeuvre' is popular in Mini servicing— accessibility is not the strongest point in the car's favour! With the link out of the way, the spring unit can be removed by releasing the compressor tool.

The lower arm can be removed without using the compressor. After the car has been lifted and placed on stands, the suspension loading is taken on the brake drum with a trolley jack and the ball pin of the lower steering swivel is freed. Releasing the shaft allows the arm to be drawn out. On replacement, tighten the nut on the shaft with the vehicle standing on its wheels to avoid preloading the rubber bushes.

At the rear of the car the spring units are mounted horizontally in a subframe which is prone to 'terminal' rust. Its renewal is outside the scope of this book, but see *How to Restore Chassis and Monocoque Bodywork* by Tommy Sandham in this series. The springs can be removed by undoing the dampers from within the body, jacking the car well clear of the ground and supporting it on stands. The end of the radius arm will fall out, releasing the 'trumpet' and its forward ball joint which can be worked out followed by the spring unit.

Rear radius-arm wear is a common fault on Minis. To rectify this, the strut should be removed as described above, the handbrake cable disconnected from the back plate and the flexible brake pipe from the radius arm. The handbrake cable sector should also be removed from the arm and the small finisher plate from the sill panel, after which the nut and the outer bracket on the end of the radius arm can be removed and the arm taken off. If a new bronze bush is needed, it must be reamed to size. New needle-roller bearings will also be needed and possibly a spindle, which must be unbolted from inside the subframe.

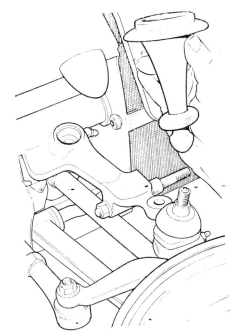

Fig. 10:2. **Removing Mini front suspension after compressing the spring and removing the link from the upper steering swivel (courtesy of Austin Rover Ltd)**

Fig. 10:3. Manoeuvring the 'trumpet' out of a Mini rear subframe

Hydrolastic suspension

In a Hydrolastic system, the front and rear suspensions are interconnected by steel piping. The system is filled with a mixture of water, alcohol and an anti-corrosion agent. Displacement of the fluid from front to rear and vice versa largely eliminates the pitching motion of the body as the car travels over uneven surfaces.

The system must be depressurized for all but the most minor suspension work, and unless you have the correct equipment for depressurizing, evacuating and repressurizing the system, you will have to call on the services of a garage. For changing displacers and pipes, the system must be evacuated to 27 in. (686 mm) of mercury. When the work has been completed, it must be refilled and pressurized. If a new displacer has been fitted, it should be 'stretched' by pressurizing to 350 or 400 psi (23 or 28 bar) for 30 minutes, after which pressure is reduced to 260 or 280 psi (18.3 or 20 bar)—the lower figures are for earlier models. Finally, the suspension height should be checked.

Chapter 11 | Wheels and tyres

The wheels and tyres are the final link between the car and the road, putting down the power, providing the braking effect and keeping the car on the chosen line when cornering.

Wheels

Three types of wheel must be considered. In terms of numbers, the pressed-steel wheel, which came into vogue in the late 1930s and has continued through to the present day, predominates. Wire wheels are something of a hangover from an earlier period. When family-car manufacturers were rapidly switching to pressed-steel wheels, only the sports-car makers stuck with the spoked wire wheel. A good wire wheel is very strong, but since it relies on the *tension* of its spokes for that strength, loose spokes spell danger. Wire wheels can and do deteriorate very rapidly if in poor condition and fitted to a powerful car. The third category is the cast-aluminium or magnesium wheel. These are light in weight and look good on certain late classics. They suffer badly from the effects of salt on the roads in winter and from brake-pad dust, which seems to embed itself and eat into the metal. A clout against a kerb or a careless tyre fitter can crack alloy wheels disastrously. All wheels should be checked carefully as part of your restoration.

In general, pressed-steel wheels give very little trouble and will last even the extended life of a restored car if kept rust free, painted and free from damage. Cracks in the centres of pressed-steel wheels were a worry on a few cars. This was mainly a problem of the 1950s and 1960s when brakes were adjusted through coinciding holes in the brake

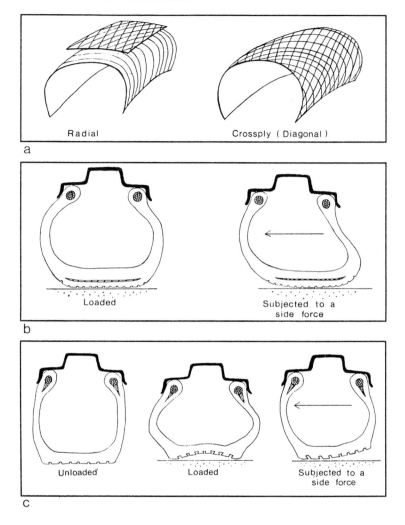

Fig. 11:1. a) Comparison of basic tyre ply structure. b) When a radial tyre is subjected to a load and to side force, the wall deflects; however, the braced tread remains open and in contact with the road. c) When a cross-ply tyre is subjected to the same loads the tread closes up, causing unreliable roadholding and premature wear (courtesy of *Thoroughbred & Classic Cars* magazine)

drums and wheels. One car which suffered in this way was the Morris Minor. To overcome the problem, later Minors had wheels without brake-adjustment holes so that they had to be removed to adjust the brakes.

A pressed-steel wheel should run true to within $\frac{1}{8}$ in. (3 mm) in both the vertical and horizontal planes. With the car jacked up, spin the wheel on a front hub (or rear hub if the car has front-wheel drive) while checking it on both sides of the rim with an improvised pointer. With the tyres off, be sure the inner flanges, on which the tyre seats, are smooth and free from rust flakes, lumps of old rubber, or badly finished welds. Tubeless tyres will remain at their correct pressures for much longer if you do so. As a final check, make sure that the tapered wheel-nut holes have not been knocked out to an enlarged, possibly oval, shape through being used with the nuts loose. If they have suffered this sort of damage, scrap the wheels.

Wire wheels can be checked for true-running in the same way but without the tyres fitted. By looking at the way the wheel is laced, you can see which spokes need tightening or easing off with a nipple key to obtain true-running in both planes. If the rim is bent, don't overtighten or slacken spokes in an effort to strain it back into line. Look for rust stains where the nipples pass through the rim; they are an infallible sign of loose spokes. Often these turn out to have been loose for some time and will resist all attempts to tighten them. You will need the help of a specialist at this stage, and you should be able to find one through the monthly classic car magazines. After respoking or trueing, any spoke heads protruding inside the rim must be filed flush. Make sure that the splines in the hubs and the tapered seats of the traditional Rudge Whitworth-type wheels are in good condition. Once these are damaged or worn, they tend to work loose continuously—not a comforting thought! Be careful with the copper hammer used to tighten the knock-on nuts of centre-lock wheels; clumsy hammering is a common cause of bent or broken spokes.

Provided they are treated with respect by tyre fitters, alloy wheels only deteriorate due to chemical attack from road salt and brake dust or damage by kerbing. Their appearance can be improved tremendously by bead-blasting and lacquering with a polyurethane lacquer.

Tyres

Radial tyres were an innovation of the 1950s and are almost universal fitments on current cars. They give much better roadholding, longer life and improved fuel economy when compared with cross-ply tyres. So is there *any* reason, other than maintaining the original specification, for fitting cross-ply tyres to an older car that is being restored?

Fig. 11:2. After removing the valve core to release the air, a tyre's bead can be broken using elementary science and a long length of wood. The block should be positioned opposite the valve

Fig. 11:3. Before attempting to remove a tyre it is essential to push the beads right into the centre of the wheel rim

Fig. 11.4. The tyre can now be eased off the rim, starting at the valve

Early arguments against radials, when they first appeared, were that they gave a harsh, noisy ride, that steering at parking speeds was heavy, and that loss of grip was more sudden and more complete when cornering than with cross-ply tyres, albeit at a much higher speed.

For the cars considered in this book, those arguments remain true, except that the violent loss of grip which, to an extent, characterized early radials has been successfully overcome. They *are* noisy on old cars, they *do* feel harsh and you can't 'drift' an early post-war sports car on radials like you can on cross-plies. True cross-plies will wear out twice as quickly as radials, but unless you intend using your classic as regular transport does it matter? On cross-ply tyres you will also use more fuel, perhaps an extra 5 per cent, but this is not a high price to pay for the comfort and correct 'period' feel that cross-plies will give. I would say fit cross-plies on pre-1962 cars. The decision is difficult with cars like the Jaguar saloons which ran from the late 1950s through to the late 1960s. Originally, they were equipped with Dunlop Road Speed cross-plies. Your choice will depend on whether you want to emphasize the comfort and luxury aspect of the car or its performance potential.

If you are restoring a relatively low-performance car, you can make sensible economies by using remoulded or retreaded tyres. In some cases, like the Morris, Ford and Standard Eights or Austin Seven which, today, probably have a maximum speed of 55–60 mph (88–96 km/h) and are not likely to be driven much over 45 mph (72 km/h), these tyres make sense if supplied by a tyre manufacturer or one of the well-known retreaders.

If, for some reason, a tyre does not quite meet new tyre standards, probably because of a moulding defect on the tread or something similar, but is perfectly safe and therefore saleable, it will have 'Remould Quality' branded on its side wall and will be sold at a remould price.

Enthusiasts owning post-war American cars might find they have bias-belted tyres and wonder where these fit into the cross-ply/radial discussion. They are a sort of 'halfway house', having a cross-ply carcass overlaid with a circumferential bracing belt like a radial. Bias-belted tyres

Fig. 11:5. Almost all limbs are needed to remove the second bead. The tyre lever pushes the bead down, the fitter's right hand pulls the tyre towards him, whilst his right foot pushes the wheel away

Fig. 11:6. When refitting a tyre you should finish at the valve, taking care not to pinch the inner tube if fitted. Incidentally, the wellies are steel-reinforced for safety

were offered early on in 'low-profile' or 'low-aspect-ratio' form, a '70 profile' tyre or one with a 70 per cent aspect ratio having a side-wall depth that is 70 per cent of its cross-section.

Wheel balancing, if carried out dynamically and accurately and preferably on the car, is always a good idea. On some cars, beginning with the first MacPherson strut-equipped Fords, it has become a necessity.

These days, most people take their cars or wheels to a tyre depot to have tyres fitted, but you might want to take off your tyres to be able to paint the wheels or to send off a set of wire wheels for respoking. What happened to the art of using tyre levers? Two things have tended to kill tyre fitting at home, both caused by the arrival of the tubeless tyre. One was the difficulty in seating the tyre beads if only a hand or foot pump was available, so you could not inflate the tyre. The other was that the tapered tyre seats or hump-based rims made unseating the tyre very difficult.

Today, the amateur restorer is likely to have a healthy air compressor which, with a full reservoir and possibly the tyre's valve core removed, will provide a strong enough blast of air to seat and seal the tyre. The second problem can be overcome by applying some extra leverage. With the wheel flat on the floor and the tyre deflated, lay a 4–5 in. (100–125 mm) block of wood on the tyre wall as near the rim as possible and away from the valve. Bear down on the block with a 3 or 4 in. (75 or 100 mm) square piece of wood about 6 ft (1.9 m) long, using a suitable fulcrum and applying your weight to the free end. This will almost always do the trick. Turn the wheel over and repeat for the other side.

When removing a tyre with levers, you must make sure that the unseated beads are pushed right into the well diametrically opposite the valve. Start about 2 in. (50 mm) from the valve, easing the tyre off the rim a little at a time. When refitting the tyres, wear a pair of stout rubber-soled boots and push and kick the tyres on with your feet, finishing at the valve.

If you want to paint the wheels without removing the tyres and, after breaking the beads away, you can see that the paint inside the rim is good, put newspaper between the tyre and the rim and lightly inflate the tyre to hold it there. This will avoid scarring the paint with tyre levers or a fitting machine and mask the tyre effectively for painting.

When fitting tyres on a high-performance car, it is important that the speed rating of the tyre is adequate for the car. The table below, compiled in conjunction with the makers of Avon tyres, shows the suitability of tyres for various speeds.

	Old Marking	Max Speeds		New Marking	Max Speeds	
		mph	km/h		mph	km/h
RADIAL	SR	113	180	P Q R S	93 99 106 113	150 160 170 180
	HR	130	210	T H	118 130	190 210
	VR	Above 130	Above 210	V	Above 130	Above 210
CROSS-PLY	None	—	—	L V	75 130	120 210

Index